Y0-CDD-301

Valentine Brobst.
Dec, 15th, 1909,
F & M academy.

3 or 4 main Points

I

2
3
4

GEORGE WASHINGTON

(From a painting by GILBERT STUART)

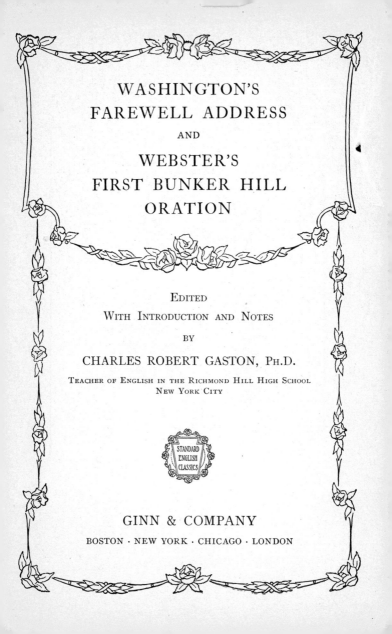

WASHINGTON'S FAREWELL ADDRESS

AND

WEBSTER'S FIRST BUNKER HILL ORATION

EDITED

WITH INTRODUCTION AND NOTES

BY

CHARLES ROBERT GASTON, Ph.D.

TEACHER OF ENGLISH IN THE RICHMOND HILL HIGH SCHOOL
NEW YORK CITY

STANDARD
ENGLISH
CLASSICS

GINN & COMPANY

BOSTON · NEW YORK · CHICAGO · LONDON

Copyright, 1906, by

CHARLES ROBERT GASTON

———————

ALL RIGHTS RESERVED

68.10

The Athenæum Press

GINN & COMPANY · PRO-
PRIETORS · BOSTON · U.S.A.

CONTENTS

INTRODUCTION

I

LIFE OF WASHINGTON THE STATESMAN

IN preparation for a careful study of Washington's great political masterpiece, his *Farewell Address to the People of the United States*, it will be best to devote most space to a consideration of his work as a statesman in the organization and successful beginning of the American nation; yet to comprehend this phase of his life fully it will be necessary to glance at the principal incidents of his earlier life in Virginia, his exploits in the French and Indian War, and his masterly guidance of the colonial troops through the Revolution.

It is hardly necessary to mention the date of Washington's birth, because February 22, 1732, is a date almost as well known as July 4, 1776. For almost a hundred years before Washington was born, his ancestors had been living in Virginia. The place of his birth was at Wakefield, in the colony of Virginia, near the shore of the Potomac River, in a parish named Washington, after the original settler of that name, John Washington, great-grandfather of George. Washington's boyhood up to the age of sixteen was spent at Wakefield or in its vicinity. He lived from 1735 to 1739 on the plantation that was later called Mount Vernon. Then the family moved to an estate nearly opposite Fredericksburg, where Washington lived till the death of his father in 1743. After this, for the rest of his boyhood, he was under the care of his mother and his half-brothers, Lawrence and Augustine. When the father's estates were divided, George went to live at

Augustine's house on the old Wakefield plantation, since that was close to a good school. Returning to his mother's home, he attended a school kept by the Rev. James Marye. The copy books he worked on have been preserved. In them are found copied in a large, round hand over a hundred maxims or rules that no doubt made a strong impression on the high-spirited Virginian boy, — rules of which this is a good specimen, "Think before you speak; pronounce not imperfectly, nor bring out your words too hastily, but orderly and distinctly." In these early school days Washington learned the rudiments of surveying. In some of his youthful papers there are neat notes of surveys and accurate geometrical figures done with the utmost care. " The end of Washington's school-days left him, if a good 'cipherer,' a bad speller, and a still worse grammarian " (P. L. Ford's *The True George Washington*).

Though living at his mother's home, Washington often visited at his brother Lawrence's plantation, Mount Vernon, where he mingled with people much older than himself. Big for his age, an expert horseman, he was a good companion for William Fairfax and Lord Fairfax, the largest property owners in Virginia. From his acquaintance with Lord Fairfax came his first real work.

In 1748, just a month after he was sixteen, Washington was chosen by Lord Fairfax to travel beyond the Blue Ridge and find out what he could about the bounds of the Fairfax estates. William Fairfax's son, George William, who was six years older than Washington, was nominally the leader in the expedition, but to Washington was assigned the actual work of surveying. The trip was not child's play, by any means, for the two friends were obliged to travel several hundred miles altogether, going and coming, and to rough it all the time. Washington acquitted himself so well in the expedition that on his return he was appointed a public surveyor by the governor of Virginia. The three years that he spent in this work hardened his frame, gave him knowledge of how to deal with difficult problems, taught him the ways of the woods, established his reputation as a reliable, absolutely accurate surveyor, and strengthened in him his early trait of silent self-dependence.

The next seven years of his life brought him into wider public notice. Lawrence Washington had been for several years interested in a land company that planned to settle emigrants in the Ohio Valley. As the French were occupying the same region, there was bound to be a clash. In preparation, the colonists of Virginia formed military organizations. Through Lawrence Washington's influence George was appointed adjutant-general, and entrusted with the work of drilling a company made up in the district that included Mount Vernon. He studied military tactics under an old soldier, took lessons in swordsmanship from a fencing-master, and commanded the company admirably. While he was staying in the island of Barbados with Lawrence, he caught the smallpox, which left him pockmarked for life. Upon the death of Lawrence in July, 1752, George became his executor. In case Lawrence's daughter should not live to be of age, George was to inherit the Mount Vernon estate. On that plantation he was now occupied for some time in settling his brother's estate. Then he once more became adjutant-general of a military district, with the rank of major. He was selected by Governor Dinwiddie as commissioner to visit the French commander in the Ohio River region, and find out why the French were building forts in English territory. This long journey began in October, 1753. The commandant was seen, an answer to the English questions was received, and the hazardous return journey accomplished. In the spring of 1754 Washington, now a lieutenant colonel, took part in his first battle, in which his force captured twenty-two prisoners and lost one man killed by the French. Colonel Washington threw up a rough fort, called Fort Necessity, which he was obliged soon to surrender on account of the appearance of a much superior force of French. He started back to Virginia on July 4, 1754, unsuccessful in his expedition, but he received the thanks of the House of Burgesses for the bravery of his soldiers and their gallant defense of their country. The next year he was with Braddock, as aide-de-camp in that general's disastrous expedition, about which everyone knows. The next three years he was energetically getting ready for another expedition against the French. During this time he made a seven weeks' journey to Boston to consult Governor Shirley and secure if he could a regular commission in the king's army. He failed in this, but in 1758 he was at the head of a Virginia regiment when the English forces occupied Fort Duquesne and gained possession of the Ohio region. These seven years from 1751 to 1758 are especially important in Washington's life because in this period he learned the necessity of meeting an enemy according to the needs of the situation rather than according to mere rules of war and old-world military tactics. Though only twenty-six years old, he had become the best known military man in America.

On January 6, 1759, Washington was married to Mrs. Martha Custis, widow of Daniel Parke Custis. He and his pretty and intelligent bride made their home at Mount Vernon, which had now become Washington's by the death of his brother Lawrence's daughter. He might have devoted the rest of his life to the busy occupation of looking after his plantations and those of his wife. He did spend the years from 1759 to 1774 in quiet domestic life at Mount Vernon, varied by the service that he gave during all this time in the Virginia House of Burgesses. He was wont to count his work as a burgess an important section of his public life, for toward the end of his *Farewell Address* he must be including his membership in the Virginia assembly when he refers to his service for his country as having lasted forty-five years. As a planter at this period, he was thoroughly posted regarding all the details of the management of his estates, from the amount of work each slave could do to the current price of tobacco. As a member of the House of Burgesses, Washington was considered by Patrick Henry "for solid information and sound judgment unquestionably the greatest man in the assembly." Though he rarely spoke, there was no question about his re-election term after term, for he was known as a thorough, faithful, well-informed worker on committees, ready to speak his opinion on important matters. In the consideration of the Stamp Act and its repeal, he showed a comprehensive grasp of the principles at stake for the colonists; so early as 1769 he wrote to a friend that he would not scruple to take arms for the gaining of American freedom if that were necessary as a last resort. This period of his life seems too ideal to be lasting. Rich, busy, respected, having a sensible, charming wife, happy in his home life and contented in the performance of his duties as vestryman and member of the assembly, he seems to have been untouched by the trials of ordinary existence. The time of stress and strain was soon to come.

In 1774 and in 1775 he was a delegate to the Continental Congresses, at Philadelphia. From June 15, 1775, till December 23, 1783, he was commander-in-chief of the Continental forces. In the Congresses he was not a speaker often appealing loudly to his fellow-members in favor of immediate force against England, but a resolute and faithful worker on committees, carrying out plans for the defense of the country and the raising of an army. At the age of forty-three he was elected by ballot in Congress as general of the Continental armies. A historian describes him at this time as a tall man of pleasing and benign countenance. His outdoor life on his plantation and his exposure to all sorts of weather and hardships during his campaigns on the frontier had given him a rugged physical strength. His strict temperance during these years helped to bring him to the perfection of physical fitness. His head was "perfectly round," his complexion florid. The most characteristic features of his countenance were his broad nostrils, his long, finely arched eyebrows, his high forehead, and his deep-set blue eyes, which looked usually earnest or even pensive. Descriptions of Washington given by friends in 1759, 1778, and 1797 all include mention of his height (6 ft., 3½ in.), his big frame, his great physical strength, and his dignified bearing.

In the war he guided the Continental forces in a masterly way familiar to all. It is sufficient here merely to enumerate his more important actions. He vigorously punished a colonel and two captains for cowardly shirking at Bunker Hill, and thus brought discipline to the army under his command. He compelled the evacuation of Boston, March 17, 1776, was defeated at the battle of Long Island on August 27, and again at White Plains on October 28 of the same year. He surprised the Hessians at Trenton December 26, 1776, and beat the British army at Princeton in January, 1777. He was defeated at Brandywine and Germantown that year, but brought the army safely through the winter of Valley Forge in 1777–1778. He fought the indecisive battle of Monmouth in 1778, and received a unanimous vote of thanks from Congress for his conduct of this action. Having passed the winter of 1779–1780 with his army near Morristown, New Jersey, he was obliged to remain on the defensive during the following year because of the weakness of his army and the insufficiency of its equipment. In 1781 he compelled the surrender of Cornwallis at Yorktown. All these achievements he accomplished, of course, not by himself alone, but assisted by the celebrated generals of the Revolution and the determined patriots of all the colonies. At last, when the war was over, he resigned as commander-in-chief, in December, 1783, at Annapolis, where Congress was then assembled. On the way there, at Fraunce's Tavern, in Broad Street, New York, he said fare-well to his officers in words which epitomize his relations with them during the war, "With a heart full of love and gratitude I now take my leave of you, most devoutly wishing that your latter days may be as prosperous and happy as your former ones have been glorious and honorable." At Annapolis he said, in delivering his resignation to Congress, "The great events, on which my resignation depended, having at length taken place, I have now the honor of offering my sincere congratula-tions to Congress, and of presenting myself before them, to sur-render into their hands the trust committed to me, and to claim the indulgence of retiring from the service of my country."

For four years after this he lived in retirement at Mount Vernon, busy with private affairs, yet necessarily thinking and planning about the best way to establish the nation securely. His farms, much neglected for eight years, needed careful management. He rejoiced in the opportunity of resuming his old, hospitable, outdoor life on a plantation. He took long journeys, much as in his earlier days, on horseback, to visit his extensive holdings of land. There was, however, a deal of correspondence to be attended to, because he was now one of the famous men of the world. People of all sorts, on all sorts of errands, visited him. Historians desired data, painters wished to make his portrait. As the nation was not yet firmly established, the man who had guided it through the war for freedom, naturally, even in retirement, gave much time to the consideration of the best means for settling the government. He understood as well as any statesman of the time the inadequacy of the Articles of Con-federation ratified in 1781. In fact, he wrote to James Warren, of Massachusetts, that the Confederation seemed little more than a shadow without substance. In furtherance of his idea of knitting the people firmly together, commercially as well as in sentiment, he planned the James River and Potomac canals. His attempts to bring about commercial union between Maryland and Virginia led to a call for a convention at Annapolis to consider the subject.

After the Annapolis convention a call was soon issued for the convention of 1787 at Philadelphia. Washington did not feel well enough to undertake attending the convention, but in spite of his pleas to be excused he was elected head of the Virginia delegation. When the convention organized, he became president. He acted as chairman during the four months of the convention, speaking only once on a motion, yet making himself a powerful influence in all the deliberations. The momentous work of forming the Constitution was consummated on September 17, 1787, on which day Washington, as presiding officer of the convention, was the first to sign the Constitution. He helped materially in getting that instrument ratified by Virginia, and when the other colonies had ratified it so that it was adopted, he was chosen President of the United States, unanimously, in February, 1789.

Washington served as President from April 30, 1789, when he was inaugurated at New York, till March 4, 1797. At the close of his first term, in 1792, he was unanimously re-elected. To forestall any efforts to induce him to serve a third term he issued, in September, 1796, his *Farewell Address to the People of the United States.*

In his address to the two houses of Congress on the day of his inauguration, Washington declared it to be his conviction that the preservation of the sacred fire of liberty and the successful perpetuation of the republican form of government depended perhaps finally on the success of the experiment then to be begun. Washington's services as first President were of incalculable worth to the nation.[1] With firmness and

[1] To these years of Washington's life, Mr. Henry Cabot Lodge, who is looking at Washington particularly from the point of view of his work

persistence a national feeling had to be nourished, or the nation could not endure. Washington was the one man in America possessed of the necessary qualifications to administer the government at its initiation. To put the machinery of national government in working order was a task of impressive magnitude when we consider the entire lack of a system upon which to build. There were no departments like those now familiar to us, no traditions, no forms of business. Funds for the expenses of government were lacking. The army was practically nothing, there was no navy. It takes a violent wrench of the thoughts to comprehend the utter absence of machinery of government when Washington set about his task. In making a start he looked for good men to assist him. No person had influence with him beyond the powers of reason and argument, said John Adams. Washington discharged the duties of his office with absolute impartiality. He made his appointments solely with a view to gathering all the talent of the country in support of the national government. Nevertheless, he advisedly chose as members of the Supreme Court and of his cabinet men who had favored the Constitution : for the Supreme Court sound lawyers like John Jay, and for the cabinet Hamilton as Secretary of the Treasury, Randolph as Attorney-General, Knox as Secretary of War, and Jefferson as Secretary of State. These were the departments which Congress established the summer after Washington's inauguration. When the work of organizing the government thus far had been completed, a good start had been made for a successful administration.

as a statesman, with justice devotes more than a third of the seven hundred pages of his biography. Other biographers, however, do not observe anything like this proportion; John Fiske, for example, in his abridgment of Irving's biography of Washington, gives less than a seventh of his six hundred pages to this period, and Horace E. Scudder allows less than an eighth of his little book of two hundred and fifty pages to Washington's life as a statesman.

1800. President Washington laid the corner-stone of the original Capitol in 1793.

The last element of the administration to be considered is the matter of the relations of the new nation with other nations. Europe was in a turmoil. The very year in which Washington was inaugurated the French Revolution broke out (see page 39). In his second term France and England were at war. Because of the aid given by France to America in the American Revolution, France expected the aid of America against England. Washington would not give it. The parties into which the people had become divided being split on the question of how to act in the crisis, it was the judgment of Washington more than any other element that kept America aloof from the European tangle. In an autograph letter now preserved in the British Museum, President Washington wrote to an English lord, from Philadelphia, under date of April 22, 1793: " I believe it is the sincere wish of united America to have nothing to do with the political intrigues or the squabbles of European nations, but on the contrary to exchange commodities and live in peace and amity with all the inhabitants of the earth." When France sent Citizen Genet to the United States in 1793 to obtain American aid, Washington checked his plans. Genet tried to get help against England from Americans who lived on the frontiers. Upon Washington's complaint to the French government, Genet was recalled.

Besides the Citizen Genet episode, another question to handle concerned the strained relations between the American nation and England. During the wars with the Indians referred to above, the English had shown themselves sympathizers with the Indians if not their secret supporters. Detroit was still held by the British soldiers, American seamen were being impressed, and ships were being seized. John Jay was sent to England, where he negotiated a treaty which partially settled the difficulties with that nation. Two of the most important items of the treaty were that it left open the question of the impressment of American seamen and that it gave to the United States the western posts long the subject of dispute. The treaty was signed late in 1794, was presented to the Senate in June of the next year for ratification, and, having been finally approved by the Senate, was signed by the President on August 18, 1795.

The conduct of these foreign complications brought upon Washington more criticism than he had ever received before since entering public life ; some critics even went so far as to say that Washington had no real merits either as a statesman or as a general. Perhaps such acerbity of denunciation prompted Washington to speak so emphatically in his *Farewell Address* regarding the need for steering clear of permanent alliances with any portion of the foreign world. Of course the sober judgment of later years, when the political animosities of the two parties of the time had been forgotten, cleared Washington entirely of the charge of blundering in the Genet and Jay incidents.

At the close of his second term in the presidency Washington again retired to Mount Vernon, having assured, so far as one great statesman could do so, the permanent prosperity of the American nation. John Jay, in a letter to Richard Peters, March 29, 1811, summed up the character of Washington's presidency concisely when he said that the administration raised the nation out of confusion into order, out of degradation and distress into reputation and prosperity : it found the country withering ; it left it flourishing.

It was with a sense of relief that Washington returned to Mount Vernon after John Adams had delivered his inaugural address as the new President. There was so much to do in repairing the buildings on his estate and looking after his farms that Washington had now no time to look into books. His letters of the period seem especially homely and interesting in their revelation of the simple life at home of a domestically inclined sexagenarian. He says the joiners and masons and painters have invaded his home, till there is hardly a room to sit in where one can escape the music of the hammer and the odoriferous scent of paint. He is almost jocular in his comments on the strange faces come out of curiosity to see him. Yet even at this late date in his life he could not be left in tranquil content, for French cruisers captured American vessels, and three members of an American commission to France were grossly insulted. The nation called Washington to the head of the army again in July, 1798. He accepted on the understanding that he should not take actual command until there should be a formal declaration of war with France. Watchful of the events happening in the nation at large, but mostly occupied with his simple home duties, he waited at Mount Vernon, ready to go to the front if actual hostilities should begin. Before the difficulty with France had been settled, he caught a severe cold on the twelfth of December from riding about his plantation "while rain, hail, and snow were falling alternately" (Ford's *The True George Washington*). He quietly passed away on December 14, 1799, and was buried at Mount Vernon.

In Washington's honor there has been erected the great Washington Monument, overlooking the Capitol and commanding a magnificent view of the city of Washington and all the surrounding country. Daniel Webster described the monument in 1851 as a "marble column, sublime in its simple grandeur, and fitly intended to reach a loftier height than any similar structure on the face of the whole earth." The monument is not now the highest structure in the world, but anyone who has seen both will at once admit that the Washington Monument is far more impressive than the Eiffel Tower of Paris, though that is almost twice as high.

Of more importance than even the grandest of marble

columns as a memorial of Washington is the esteem in which he has been held, in America and the civilized world, since the day of his death. For several years preceding the death of Washington celebrations of his birthday were held in various patriotic circles. Since then the observance of this anniversary has become universal. Hundreds of commemorative addresses delivered on February 22, in praise of Washington, have been printed and widely circulated. One of the most notable occasions on which his virtues and services were commemorated was the centennial anniversary in the city of Washington, when Daniel Webster eulogized the " Father of his Country." With a paragraph from that eloquent memorial oration this sketch of Washington's life may be concluded. The tribute of Webster is worth being committed to memory.

" We are met here to testify our regard for him whose name is intimately blended with whatever belongs most essentially to the prosperity, the liberty, the free institutions, and the renown of our country. That name was of power to rally a nation, in the hour of thick-thronging public disasters and calamities; that name shone, amid the storm of war, a beacon light, to cheer and guide the country's friends; it flamed, too, like a meteor, to repel her foes. That name, in the days of peace, was a loadstone, attracting to itself a whole people's confidence, a whole people's love, and the whole world's respect. That name, descending with all time, spreading over the whole earth, and uttered in all the languages belonging to the tribes and races of men, will forever be pronounced with affectionate gratitude by every one in whose breast there shall arise an aspiration for human rights and human liberty."

QUESTIONS

1. Which do you consider the more interesting, Washington's early life or his life after 1775?

2. Was Washington an educated man?

Circumstances of the Composition and Publication of the Farewell Address

When Washington accepted the presidency in 1789, he had no idea of occupying the office more than one term. As the end of his term approached, he gave his thoughts to the question of how he might announce his intention not to serve longer. On 20 May, 1792, he wrote to James Madison asking for advice on the subject. In this letter Washington reiterated what he had said to Madison in various conversations, — that he wished to retire from office in order that he might spend the remainder of his days, which he could not expect to be long, in ease and tranquillity. A part of the letter was occupied by a proposed valedictory address evidently mapped out after much reflection on the matter. Madison was requested to offer suggestions on what he deemed suitable to include in such an address — if it was thought advisable to prepare a farewell. He replied on 20 June, 1792, offering a rough draft beginning, " The period which will close the appointment with which my fellow-citizens have honored me, being not very distant, and the time actually arrived at which their thoughts must be designating the citizen who is to administer the executive government of the United States during the ensuing term, it may be requisite to a more distinct expression of the public voice, that I should apprise such of my fellow-citizens as may retain their partiality towards me, that I am not to be numbered among those out of whom a choice is to be made." It will be noticed that in the final address Washington retained this sentence substantially as proposed by Madison. In this letter Madison gave as his advice regarding the mode of publication of the address Washington wished to make, that there was no better mode than " a simple publication in the newspapers," because there

would be no opportunity of offering it through the medium
of the general legislature, and the situation would hardly admit
of a recurrence to the state governments which were the
channels used for the former valedictory address known among
Washington's writings as *General Washington's Address to
the Governors of the States on Disbanding the Army.* The
precedent at Washington's military exit made it wise, in
Madison's opinion, to publish some kind of farewell at the
laying down of the duties of the presidency.

Washington's desire to leave the official service of the
government at this time, however, had to yield for another
four years to his sense of his duty to the nation. Consequently he accepted another term. As the end of this second
term drew near, he again made up his mind that he should be
allowed to retire to private life, though there seemed to be
a general desire on the part of the people that he accept still
another term. In May, 1796, toward the close of his second
term, he received from Alexander Hamilton a request that
a proposed draft of a farewell address be sent to Hamilton in
order that he might do as the President had asked him in con-
versation to do, namely, suggest ideas to be included in the
address. For most of the time intervening between this date
and the date of publication both Washington and Hamilton
had the subject on their minds. A number of letters passed
between them with regard to the points to be covered and
their proper expression. Jay also was consulted by the President on the important subject. A letter of John Jay, written
March 29, 1811, to explain the history of the composition
of the address, is of especial value in a determination of how
the address was formed. The material parts of the letter
follow : —

"Some time before the address appeared, Colonel, (afterwards General), Hamilton, informed me that he had received
a letter from President Washington, and with it the draft of a

Farewell Address, which the President had prepared, and on which he requested our opinion. He then proposed that we should fix on a day for an interview at my house on the subject. A day was accordingly appointed, and on that day Colonel Hamilton attended. He observed to me in words to this effect, that after having read and examined the draft, it appeared to him to be susceptible of improvement. That he thought the easiest and best way was to leave the draft, untouched, and in its fair state; and to write the whole over with such amendments, alterations, and corrections as he thought were advisable, and that he had done so; he then proposed to read it and make it the subject of our consideration. This being agreed to, he read it, and we proceeded deliberately to discuss and consider it, paragraph by paragraph, until the whole met with our mutual approbation. Some amendments were made during the interview, but none of much importance.

"Although this business had not been hastily dispatched, yet, aware of the consequence of such a paper, I suggested the giving it further critical examination; but he declined it, saying he was pressed for time, and was anxious to return the draft to the President without delay.

"It afterwards occurred to me that a certain proposition was expressed in terms too general and unqualified; and I hinted it in a letter to the President. As the business took the course above mentioned, a recurrence to the draft was unnecessary, and it was not read. There was this advantage in the course pursued; the President's draft remained, (as delicacy required,) fair and not obscured by interlineations, &c. By comparing it with the paper sent with it, he would immediately observe the particular emendations and corrections, that were proposed, and would find them standing in their intended places. Hence he was enabled to review, and to decide on the whole matter, with much greater clearness and facility, than if he had received them in separate and detached notes, and with detailed references to the page and lines, where they were advised to be introduced" (*Memoirs of the Historical Society of Pennsylvania*, Vol. I, Part II, pp. 249–251).

The draft made by Hamilton and discussed by him with Jay is printed as an appendix in Horace Binney's *An Inquiry into the Formation of Washington's Farewell Address*, Philadelphia, 1859. Here a number of passages proposed by Hamilton but not finally embodied by Washington in his address are enclosed in brackets. Though a minute study of the origin of Washington's great state paper is intensely fascinating, it reveals for general purposes only this, that Washington, before giving to the country an important state paper, desired, like most great executives, all possible advice, obtained it, and then followed in the main the dictates of his own matured judgment.

Regarding the manner in which the address was first made public, David C. Claypoole wrote a detailed and convincing statement, dated February 22, 1826, and published in the *Memoirs of the Historical Society of Pennsylvania*, Vol. I, Part II, pp. 255–257. He says that a few days before the appearance of the document in print he received a message from the secretary of the President, requesting him to call upon the President. The President received him privately, in his drawing-room, and explained that he had for some time contemplated retiring from public life; that he had some thoughts and reflections which he wished to communicate to the people of the United States, in the form of an address, to appear in the columns of the *American Daily Advertiser*, of which Mr. Claypoole was editor and proprietor. Of course the editor thanked President Washington for having chosen his paper as the channel through which the communication should be made. It was then arranged that the manuscript should be taken by the President's secretary to the printer on the next day, which was Friday, and that the publication should be on the following Monday. After the President had corrected the proof, making few alterations from the original except in the punctuation, " in which he was very minute," the address was printed, on the day agreed upon, September 19, 1796. However, the editor of the *Advertiser* seems to have taken it upon himself to date the address September 17, 1796, in spite of the fact that the original manuscript, in Washington's own hand, presented by him to Claypoole after the publication of the document, and now preserved in the Lenox Library, New York, is plainly dated United States, 19th September, 1796, the day fixed upon in advance, by the President, for publication. There was no issue of the paper on Sunday, the eighteenth, and very likely the type was set up on the seventeenth. I conjecture, therefore, that the date of the putting of the address into type is the date usually given for the address, namely, September 17, 1796. This statement of the circumstances leading directly to the publication will at all events show plainly how the confusion in dates arose.

On September the twentieth, the day after the document was printed, the *Advertiser* contained a little paragraph : "Yesterday morning the President of the United States left this city [Philadelphia], on his journey to Mount Vernon." In the issues of the newspaper immediately preceding the publication of the great state paper, there is no intimation that the address would soon be published, nor are there comments upon it in subsequent issues.

II

LIFE OF WEBSTER THE ORATOR

DANIEL WEBSTER (Jan. 18, 1782–Oct. 24, 1852) was forty-three years old when he delivered the oration popularly known as the *First Bunker Hill Oration*. At this time, June 17, 1825, he had been before the public for almost a quarter of a century as a speaker of magnetic power and eloquence. He had gained fame as one of the stanchest upholders of national development and unity. He was the idol of New England in politics and law. Only the year before, he had been elected to the 19th Congress by a vote of four thousand nine hundred and ninety out of five thousand votes cast. He had already delivered orations considered at the time among the finest ever spoken in New England. All this success had not come by chance. His school and college days prepared him generously for the eminent position he had gained in the practice of the law and the pursuit of politics; his experiences in the courts and the legislature fitted him for his occasional extraordinary bursts of oratory such as the Bunker Hill oration.

Like Hawthorne and Scott, Johnson and Pope, Webster was delicate as a boy, and unable to attend school regularly. The good women of his native town, Salisbury, New Hampshire, were sure so delicate a child would never live to grow up. He loved to play in the woods and fields and to read good books. Addison's essays in *The Spectator* were favorites with him in these early days. An old soldier used to carry him about on his back and tell him stories of Bunker Hill and the deeds of the armies. The teamsters used to talk in tones of wonderment of what that " Webster boy " knew, picked up hit or miss from his reading, and they used to like to hear him read the Bible, says one of his biographers, because the boy read with an extraordinary childish eloquence. He knew by heart large portions of the Holy Scriptures, and learned most of the Constitution of the United States from studying one side of a bandanna handkerchief containing that masterpiece of political wisdom. His attendance at district schools here and there was not of much moment in the progress of his education. It was not till he reached the age of fourteen that he began school work of any real significance. In 1796 he entered Phillips Exeter Academy, a diffident boy averse to public performances of any kind. It was impossible to get him to appear before the school when it was his turn to declaim. After less than a year at the academy, his father and mother, though poor, resolved to put another mortgage on the farm, wear their old clothes another season, and let Daniel go to college. He was consequently placed under the instruction of a minister who coached him sufficiently in Latin and Greek for him to enter Dartmouth College, at Hanover, New Hampshire.

In August, 1797, he entered college. Here he found himself ill prepared in the classics and disinclined to the study of mathematics. In this respect there is something very human about young Webster. He was not one of your youthful prodigies of all-round learning. Yet by strict attention to the work in hand, he made up the deficiencies of his preparation, so that by the end of his Freshman year he was recognized as the best student of his class. Moreover, as he grew older he lost the diffidence that had been due to his realization of how much like a farmer's boy he looked in comparison with some of his schoolmates. He became, indeed, a good college declaimer, and he made a little money to help pay his college expenses by editing a weekly paper for a year. In 1800 he was called upon to deliver the Fourth of July oration before the citizens of Hanover. Though somewhat bombastic, as was to be expected from his youth and training, this speech, the first of Webster's orations that has been preserved, gave promise of his later more truly oratorical addresses. After four years in college, he received his degree in 1801.

Upon graduating he commenced the study of the law in the office of a successful lawyer of Salisbury. He found, however, that there was no money in the lawyer's office. He desired money now not so much for his own enjoyment as for the success of his brother's plans. Ezekiel, who was older than Daniel, had made up his mind also to go to college. As school teaching promised greater immediate returns than a law office, Daniel taught school in Fryeburg, Maine. He made a good school-teacher, liked by the boys and the villagers. Then he resumed work in the lawyer's office. When he came of age, he joined the church. His interest in politics also began to be keen, the Federalist party being the one which attracted his support. In 1804 he went to Boston, where he continued his legal education. The next year he was admitted to the bar, at the age of twenty-three.

From the time of his admission to the bar till his election to Congress, Webster was busy in the practice of the law. He soon outgrew Boscawen, where, after admission to the bar, he started his practice, and moved to a larger place, Portsmouth, the chief town of his native state, the same place celebrated for the arranging of the Peace of Portsmouth, between Japan and Russia, in 1905. He became known as a skilled practitioner who had a faculty for eloquent speech on occasion. It was not long before he could hold his own fairly well with the most eminent lawyer of New Hampshire, Jeremiah Mason, a man much older than he. It is recorded, however, that though Mr. Mason greatly admired the talents of his young opponent and ungrudgingly praised them, it was Mr. Mason who won the cases when the two men were pitted against

each other. Incidentally Webster continued to show his oratorical bent in Fourth of July orations and addresses on patriotic themes. His style was vivid and fluent, though a little
too sophomoric for greatest effectiveness in winning cases in
the courts. His anniversary address of July 4, 1806, before
the Federal gentlemen of Concord, New Hampshire, and its
vicinity, is characterized by such cutting irony and so much of
righteous sarcasm that it stirs one's feelings even when read in
the deep quiet of the British Museum on a summer's day.
" Patriotism hath given place," says the young orator, " to the
more laudable spirit of economy. Regard to national honor,
that remnant of chivalry, and offspring of the dark ages, is
absorbed in a thirst for gain and desire of saving — the liberal
sentiments of enlightened times." By studying the methods
of opponents like Mason, he learned that when he was in a
court room he ought to prune his natural flights, speak more
directly, and thus appeal more surely to juries. As a lawyer
in Portsmouth, Webster developed steadily and rapidly, being
distinguished principally by a certain intolerant rudeness of
strength, an impressive indolence of manner until aroused,
and a quality of seizing upon the essential principles under-
lying the cases which he argued.

His Fourth of July oration in 1812 at Portsmouth before
the Washington Benevolent Society was considered remarkable
at the time. Published at Portsmouth that year, it was read
widely through the New England states. In fact, it was the
immediate cause of his entrance into active political life. For
three or four years previous to this time he had felt a strong
inclination for politics, and had been pointed to by his friend,
the shrewd-minded lawyer who later became governor, Mr.
William Plumer, as especially fitted for this kind of service to
the state. As a result of the favor with which his Portsmouth
speech was received, Webster was elected a delegate to the
Rockingham County convention in August, 1812. In this

convention he was chosen to write a memorial condemning the war with England. The memorial that Webster produced was a remarkably strong presentation of the current Federalist sentiment. It was so much to the taste of the Rockingham County delegates that Webster was selected by the convention as the nominee for Congress, and it was so much approved by the voters that he was easily elected. In the national House of Representatives Webster made few speeches during this first term of his, in the 13th Congress, because he was feeling his way and reading and reflecting on the questions of moment in this critical period. One of his speeches in the Congress was his address in 1814 on a bill making further provision for filling the ranks of the regular army. Webster maintained that public policy demanded strengthening and expansion of the navy rather than the army. At the close of his term he was elected again, and now spoke more frequently.

His efforts in favor of a sound, conservative national bank were his most important work in this session. His eloquent speeches were constantly referred to in conversations among the members, for he had already become a leading member of the House.

In 1816 Webster moved to Boston, declining another nomination to Congress. For six years he made his home quietly in Boston, though he was often called to Washington to argue cases before the Supreme Court. Instead of the income of two thousand dollars which had been all he could make up to this time, he soon found himself making twenty thousand in this wider field. He was even at this period of his life, however, so careless in money matters that he never saved any money; before his death he had to face charges of dishonesty in the handling of public funds, because his early carelessness became later a habit never overcome. One of the reasons for his political retirement at this period was no doubt his great grief over the death of his daughter

Grace. The dignified lawyer and statesman was completely broken down with sorrow over the death of a child whom he dearly loved.

During this intermission in his political career Webster made his most famous legal argument, that in the Dartmouth College case, before the Supreme Court. There is scarcely space in a biographical sketch of this length to take more than a passing glance at the connection of Webster with this case. In his interesting and lucid exposition of the facts of the great legal controversy, in the American Statesmen biography of Webster, Mr. Henry Cabot Lodge points out that Webster won the case for his alma mater not altogether on his strong constitutional argument, but also to a large extent on the strength of other elements in his speeches that dealt with matters outside the law. Briefly, the circumstances of the case were that there were two boards of trustees of the college, one elected by those representing the founders of the institution and the other by the New Hampshire legislature. The college trustees held that the board appointed by the legislature could not legally serve. The case finally came before the Supreme Court of the United States. Webster was the principal lawyer for the plaintiffs. He made his argument March 10, 1818. By his masterly arrangement of the legal points gathered by other lawyers associated with him, and by his skillful and supremely tactful appeal to the political prejudices of Chief Justice Marshall and the other judges, Webster gained their sympathy so that they decided in favor of the college trustees.

After the period of political inactivity Webster was again called to Congress. In 1822, without any solicitation on his part, he was elected to represent Massachusetts in the lower House. In this Congress he made a number of striking speeches, as, for example, the one delivered in April, 1824, in opposition to a protective tariff measure advocated by Henry

Clay. In support of an administration measure strongly urged by President John Quincy Adams, Webster delivered another important speech, in which he ably expounded the so-called Monroe doctrine. Still, Webster's most valuable work in Congress at this time was his carrying through a measure by which the whole body of the criminal law of the United States was codified, — a measure in the preparation of which he had the wise and learned assistance of another great lawyer, Judge Story.

Although during this engrossing period of his life his time was laboriously occupied with matters of legislation, his general interest in patriotic subjects continued, and he gave utterance to eloquent expressions on such topics on several special occasions. Four such addresses were delivered in the years 1820, 1824, 1825, and 1826. On December 22, 1820, three days before the anniversary, he delivered a polished oration at Plymouth in commemoration of the two hundredth anniversary of the landing of the Pilgrims. The address was published in 1821 in Boston. This oration was regarded by Webster's contemporaries as the most eloquent address ever spoken on the American continent. Later judgment, however, generally awards this honor to another speech of Webster's, yet without detracting from the eloquence of the Plymouth oration. The subject is a sketch of the events that made the United States a nation. The broad field chosen by the orator was peculiarly adapted to show his remarkable powers of brilliant utterance on national themes. The second of these addresses, though not strictly an occasional speech, is interesting because it shows Webster's love for his own country widening to include consideration for the welfare of another land. In the same year in which Byron was giving his life for the principle of freedom for the Greeks, and only a few years before Tennyson hurried to Spain to do what he could in aid of revolutionists there, Webster's thoughts also were including a far-away nation, though it is not recorded that he personally assisted by money or presence, as did Byron and Tennyson. At any rate, there was published in Washington in 1824, and widely translated soon thereafter in Europe, Webster's patriotic speech on the Greek Revolution, delivered in Congress, January 19, 1824. This eloquent speech was occasioned by the struggles of the Greeks, and was ostensibly in support of Webster's resolution providing for the expenses of an American commissioner to Greece, yet it really was an exposition of a broader theme, — the national destiny of the United States with regard to other nations. In the words of Webster, "I close, then, Sir, with repeating that the object of this resolution is to avail ourselves of the interesting occasion of the Greek Revolution, to make our protest against the doctrines of the Allied Powers; both as they are laid down in principle, and as they are applied in practice." The third of these occasions was the laying of the corner-stone of the Bunker Hill Monument. The oration delivered on June 17, 1825, needs no comment in this place. It ranks as oratory higher than either of the others just mentioned, great as they are. The last of the four, the address of 1826, was the eulogy on Adams and Jefferson, containing a famous passage on eloquence which deserves to be quoted here: "Clearness, force, and earnestness are the qualities which produce conviction. True eloquence, indeed, does not consist in speech. It cannot be brought from far. Labor and learning may toil for it, but they will toil in vain. Words and phrases may be marshaled in every way, but they cannot compass it. It must exist in the man, in the subject, and in the occasion. Affected passion, intense expression, the pomp of declamation, all may aspire to it: they cannot reach it. It comes, if it come at all, like the outbreaking of a fountain from the earth, or the bursting forth of volcanic fires, with spontaneous, original, native force. The graces taught in the schools, the costly ornaments and studied contrivances of speech, shock and disgust men, when their own lives and the fate of their wives, their children, and their country hang on the decision of the hour. Then words have lost their power, rhetoric is vain, and all elaborate oratory contemptible. Even genius itself then feels rebuked and subdued, as in the presence of higher qualities. Then patriotism is eloquent; then self-devotion is eloquent. The clear conception, outrunning the deductions of logic, the high purpose, the firm resolve, the dauntless spirit, speaking on the tongue, beaming from the eye, informing every feature, and urging the whole man onward, right onward to his object, — this, this is eloquence; or rather it is something greater and higher than all eloquence, — it is action, noble, sublime, godlike action." These four representative orations of Webster, then, indicate that in the press of legislative duties at this period he still had time to continue his interest in broad national themes and to make stirring commemorative speeches.

The ill health of Senator E. H. Mills, of Massachusetts, made it necessary for that state to consider who should be chosen as his successor. All eyes turned to Webster. When the vacancy came, he was elected by the state legislature as senator from Massachusetts, and accepted the office in June, 1827. His election to the Senate closes the first half of his experience in national politics. Under fifty years of age, he was now a leader among men prominent in political life. He stood so high in the eyes of the people of his time, that if his life had ended then he might have been remembered for generations as a great speaker on national subjects on special occasions, and as a legislator who stood at all times for the unity and progress of his country.

To the student of the political history of the United States Webster's mature years in the Senate and the cabinet furnish more elements of interest than anything narrated in the preceding sketch; but to those who are looking at Webster rather as the greatest of American commemorative orators, these years from 1827 to 1852 are not so important. In short compass, the more important facts of Webster's career during these years as United States Senator and Secretary of State may be related, and the further contributions which he made to oratorical literature may be explained, sufficiently for the purpose in mind. The subject divides itself into four headings: 1. Entrance to Senate and first period there; 2. Secretary of State; 3. Return to Senate; 4. Secretary of State the second time.

During his first period in the Senate (1827–1841), Webster won his greatest fame by his celebrated reply to Hayne. On Tuesday and Wednesday, January 26 and 27, 1830, in answer to a speech by Mr. Robert Young Hayne, of South Carolina, Webster delivered a speech which has probably been more often drawn upon for quotations and selected declamations than any other American speech. Senator Samuel A. Foote, of Connecticut, toward the end of the preceding month, had introduced the following seemingly harmless resolution: "Resolved, That the Committee on Public Lands be instructed to inquire and report the quantity of public lands remaining unsold within each State and Territory, and whether it be expedient to limit for a certain period the sales of the public lands to such lands only as have heretofore been offered for sale, and are now subject to entry at the minimum price. And, also, whether the office of surveyor-general, and some of the land offices may not be abolished without detriment to the public interest." Senator Hayne took occasion to point out the hostility of the East to the growing West, shown in Foote's resolution. Senator Webster replied, in a strong speech, denying that any hostility had been shown to the West. Hayne returned to the charge, going afield from the main point at issue, and enlarging upon the doctrine that the Federal government is not the exclusive judge of how far the powers of the nation extend over the states. Hayne's is by no means an insignificant speech, for it reads well to-day if one considers merely its form and tone. Yet Webster overwhelmed Hayne oratorically in a second answer, spoken partly on a Tuesday and finished the next day. This speech is the noblest of expositions of what the Constitution and the Union meant to the people of the North and the West in 1830; it is Webster's greatest political address.

Other important speeches of Webster in the Senate at this period were those on the constitutionality of the United States bank, on the Subtreasury plan, and on the South Carolina Ordinance of nullification.

During this long period in the Senate, Webster was in the forefront of every political controversy. However, he found time early in his first term to take part in the White murder trial, in 1831, making a marvelously vivid argument for the prosecution. Toward the end of his first period in the Senate, Webster felt the need of rest, and journeyed to England and France, where he spent some months in 1839. Two years later he resigned from the Senate to enter the cabinet.

Upon the election of William H. Harrison as President, Webster accepted the office of Secretary of State in 1841, and held this place in the cabinet through the short, one-month term of Harrison and through part of the term of Tyler, until May, 1843, when for a year he retired to private life and his law practice. The principal diplomatic difficulty that Webster had to meet when he was Secretary of State in these administrations was the question of the northeastern boundary. There were so many complicating features in the international politics of the era that it looked as if there would certainly be war; but England finally sent to the United States as boundary commissioner a man who had coolness of judgment and understanding of the question, Lord Ashburton. With him Webster arranged a satisfactory settlement of the trouble. In spite of the great difficulty in getting the confirmation of the Senate in this country and of Parliament in England, Webster and Lord Ashburton finally carried the treaty through, and the boundary was thus settled without war. This is Webster's most important achievement as head of the cabinet during Tyler's term, though he acquitted himself in statesmanlike fashion in handling several minor problems, such as the making of a treaty with Portugal and the vindication of the course of the United States in the matter of the gaining of independence by Texas. In 1844 Webster was re-elected Senator from Massachusetts.

While serving in the Senate again Webster was from time to time talked about as a presidential possibility. He was too big a man to be President in those days. He was not enough of a politician and he was too much of a statesman. There were always hindrances in his way at nominating conventions, yet he longed to be President. Perhaps it was because of this longing that he gradually shifted ground with regard to what was now a burning question, slavery. At any rate, though he opposed with tremendous force in his earlier speeches, from 1819 to about 1840, the principle of slavery and the specific extension of it under the Constitution, he came in 1850 to the lukewarm attitude which produced the memorable utterance known as the Seventh of March Speech. As a party man, he had hesitated to put himself at the head of a new party when the Whigs with whom he was allied wavered on the question of slavery; yet he was loath to join the Free-Soilers, who were more decided in their opposition. Thus, sticking to his party, he was led to what men of the North consider his great blunder as a statesman. In his Seventh of March Speech he endeavored to win the North to believe that a compromise with the South on the question of slavery was for the best interests of the nation. He saw that the forces of the two sections would clash before long unless matters should be compromised. He tried to stem the feeling of the North against the extension of slavery and against the return of fugitive slaves. Since he aimed at what is now seen to have been the impossible, he failed in this speech to accomplish his object.

Again Webster resigned from the Senate to become Secretary of State, this time under President Fillmore. He entered the cabinet in July, 1850, at the age of sixty-eight. The best of his life was behind him. Still, his great intellectual powers were sufficient to enable him to perform the necessary cabinet duties with acumen and skill. Several delicate problems requiring statesmanship of a high order had to be handled at this period, such as the unpleasantness with Austria on account of the sympathy in the United States for the Hungarian revolutionist, Kossuth, the correspondence with the English minister regarding the neutrality of the proposed Nicaraguan canal, the invasion of Cuba in which volunteers from the United States took part, bringing about difficulties with Spain almost resulting in war, and the disputes with England regarding the fisheries. These problems occupied Webster's thoughts and drew from him a number of able dispatches in the last summer of his life. As a presidential convention approached, his friends again put him forward for the nomination, but in the convention he received few votes, so that one more disappointment embittered his last year. In May, 1852, he was thrown from his carriage while driving near his farm at Marshfield, Massachusetts. Together with the disease which had already weakened his constitution, the injury sustained in the fall from his carriage made recovery improbable. He lingered on, however, till October 24, 1852, when he died at three o'clock in the morning at his Marshfield home by the sea. His last words of consciousness were, "I still live."

This sentence may be considered prophetic. The greatest of American orators, the leader of the Senate for a quarter of a century, the lawyer who held the foremost place at the bar for over thirty years, and the statesman who during that time more than any other statesman, in season and out of season, vigorously and skillfully upheld the principle of national unity, dignity, and power, Daniel Webster must remain for all years a towering personality in American history. One cannot love him, because he was too proud. One cannot revere him, because he lacked moral strength. Yet one cannot help admiring him for his wonderful powers of mind and his transcendent genius as an orator. No one can read the polished, perfected utterances of Daniel Webster on the destiny of our nation without feeling the bright glow of patriotism. His words still live.

QUESTIONS

1. What is there that is specially significant in Webster's school and college life?
2. How did he first make his mark in the world?
3. What is his most celebrated law case?
4. What was his career as a statesman?
5. What were his most striking characteristics as a man?
6. What are some of his great commemorative speeches?

The Occasion, the Oration, and the Battle

As a means of giving one the best appreciation of what Daniel Webster's *First Bunker Hill Oration* is, it is worth while to reflect upon matters connected with the delivery of the speech, upon the most important characteristics of the speaker and his oration, and upon the circumstances of the battle commemorated by the monument.

An Address delivered at the Laying of the Corner Stone of the Bunker Hill Monument is the description of the famous oration as it appears on the title-page of the first edition, a thin octavo volume, published in Boston in 1825. This description shows the circumstance which produced the address. So early as December, 1794, there had been erected on the hill by Masonic brethren of General Joseph Warren, who was killed in the conflict, a monument in his honor. Then, some twenty years later, a number of patriotic gentlemen of Boston decided to build a monument to commemorate fittingly the battle itself. For this purpose an association was formed, with General John Brooks, a Bunker Hill veteran, as the first president. The second president was Daniel Webster. Through a great deal of correspondence, the project made considerable headway. (See *The History of the Bunker Hill Monument Association during the First Century of the United States of America*, by George Washington Warren, a copy of which is to be found in the building at the base of the monument.) The approach of the fiftieth anniversary of the engagement seemed a most appropriate time for starting the actual work of construction. Moreover, General Lafayette, who was at this time making a tour of the states, and was everywhere receiving welcome, promised to be present at the laying of the corner-stone. The occasion thus became one of national interest. As president of the association Webster was requested by the trustees to make the principal address.

Invitations to be present were sent to all living veterans who had taken part in the battle and to all Revolutionary soldiers within reach. Forty of the veterans who fought in the battle attended the laying of the corner-stone of the monument, and about two hundred other Revolutionary soldiers were also present (Richard Frothingham's *History of the Siege of Boston and of the Battles of Lexington, Concord, and Bunker Hill. Also an Account of the Bunker Hill Monument*). Provision was made by the Massachusetts legislature for the payment of the expenses of these honored soldiers. Lafayette of course was a prominent invited guest. Another guest of distinction was the Grand Master of the Free-Masons. There were also in attendance delegations from states adjoining Massachusetts, from New York and other Middle Atlantic states, and even from some of the Southern states, remote as they were before the days of express trains. Naturally the citizens of Boston gathered by thousands to be stirred by the ceremonies; residents who could not get within hearing posted themselves on roofs, towers, or heights overlooking the scene. The procession started from the State House in Boston early in the morning of June 17, a cool, clear day, when the weather was ideal for an outdoor programme. The procession marched in the following order: A military escort, the members of the Bunker Hill Monument Association, the brethren of the Masonic fraternity in full regalia, Lafayette and other invited guests, and a long array of societies with badges and banners. By the time the end of the procession was leaving the State House the front was almost at Charlestown Bridge. In fact, there were twenty thousand spectators gathered at Breed's Hill when the ceremonies began.

The services at Breed's Hill opened with the laying of the corner-stone by the Grand Master of the Free-Masons, John Abbot, assisted by General Lafayette, who spread the cement over the stone. Part of the service consisted of a prayer by Rev. Joseph Thaxter, chaplain of Colonel Prescott's regiment in 1775, who had prayed for the colonial soldiers just before the opening of the engagement. There was also the reading of an ode by Rev. John Pierpont. In the corner-stone were placed five different accounts of the battle, plans of the engagement and of Charlestown, an address and letter connected with the Monument Association, Edward Everett's oration on the Battle of Lexington, specimens of Continental currency, coins and medals of the United States, a fragment of Plymouth Rock, and copies of the Boston papers published during the week of the celebration. Then, on the northern slope of the hill, the multitude gathered to hear Webster's oration. On the stage with the speaker were the chief guests and the Revolutionary soldiers.

Webster was chosen as the principal speaker, it has been intimated above, because he was president of the Bunker Hill Monument Association. There were, however, a number of other considerations which no doubt determined the selection. One reason was, very likely, because it was well understood that his physical appearance always commanded the enthusiasm of an audience. When he was speaking he seemed eight feet tall; yet he was only five feet ten. His head was like a dome; his eyes were coals of fire. Carlyle, in a letter to Emerson, describes the eyes as "dull black eyes under the precipice of brows, like dull anthracite furnaces needing only to be blown," and characterizes the mouth as a "mastiff mouth." In 1839, on a visit to Liverpool, Webster was walking along the street one day when someone set up the cry, "There goes a king," and everybody gazed at Webster in wonder. People often called him a god, in their enthusiasm at his striking appearance. Again, his voice would carry far in the open air. It was a quiet voice, rarely raised to a point where the orator seemed exerting himself, yet its carrying powers were remarkable. Moreover, it was a pleasing voice, one that rested an audience. The tones were sometimes low and musical. At times the deep reverberating sounds were like "the richness of an organ." In writing of his powers of voice and manner as an orator, it is hard to refrain from using such words as splendid and magnificent. Why not admit at once that the effect was just this? Even when one who has no pretensions to oratorical skill reads aloud an oration of Webster he finds his voice inevitably expanding, and splendid seems to be about the only word that fits what one feels sure must have been the manner of Webster in uttering the oration. Webster never played the orator, or seemed to be making effort. People did not think of the manner of speaking till the address was finished. His whole bearing when in repose or action was immensely impressive. It is related that he never punished his children, as other parents have done; with him a look of reproof was enough, whether he dealt with children or men. In his preface to a collection of Webster's masterpieces, the

Rev. Mr. Tefft describes the oratory as having been calm, slow, dignified, and unambitious, yet direct and powerful. Finally, the achievements in oratory which had already given Webster a mighty New England reputation were also a consideration involved in his selection as orator of the day. The trustees confidently counted on his repeating or eclipsing his former triumphs at Portsmouth and Plymouth. This expectation was fulfilled.

In the case of a man endowed by nature with such extraordinary powers of personal magnetism and voice, it might be thought that the oration itself would seem insignificant when closely examined. Such is not the fact. In his fascinating paper, *A Trip to England*, Goldwin Smith makes the assertion that American oratory almost always savors somewhat of the school of elocution, and has the fatal drawback of being felt to aim at effect. With regard to Webster this would at first sight seem to be true, for he unquestionably had great dramatic power. It was said of him early in life that he had in him the making of an actor of the first rank. When in his reply to Hayne, at the close of his eloquent references to the patriotism of Massachusetts, he turned dramatically and faced the friends from home, the effect was so great that they "shed tears like girls." Yet such acts as these were not mere oratorical tricks; they were an essential accomplishment of the man, to get an effect without knowing just how, or caring, and without making the hearer conscious that an emotional effect was desired.

The *First Bunker Hill Oration* is the best example of occasional oratory. This kind of public speaking has been defined as the form of address which takes an anniversary, a great historical event or character, a celebration, or occasion of any sort, as a starting point, and permits close adherence to the text or the widest latitude of treatment. The occasional address is sometimes called patriotic oratory when it deals with a great national event. One of the commonest forms of occasional oration is that which may be called commemorative. In prose oral composition, the commemorative oration corresponds to the elegy of written poetical composition, of which *Lycidas* of Milton and *In Memoriam* of Tennyson are examples. The special difference, besides the difference of prose on the one hand and poetry on the other, is that the commemorative oration deals principally with events important in a nation's history, while the elegy deals with the death of a lamented man whose loss gives the poet sorrow. The elegy is fittingly composed in a churchyard under a centuries-old yew tree; the commemorative oration is produced at its best under the inspiration of the sympathetic presence of throngs of patriots. The actual composition may be performed beforehand, as in the case of Webster's *Bunker Hill,* but the first effectiveness of the occasional, commemorative oration depends largely on the spirit of the hearers assembled for the occasion. In oratory of this character the speaker must not resort to mere vague generalizations and solemn statements in commonplace form of what everyone knows, but he must raise the theme to the dignity it deserves. An analysis of the Bunker Hill address shows that Webster did not fail on this occasion to meet the tests for good commemorative oratory.

The theme, stated broadly, is the significance of the Battle of Bunker Hill to Webster's hearers. A synopsis of the oration, section by section, might be made as follows: More important in the history of our country and rousing greater feelings in men of our day than the discovery of America by Columbus or the settlement by English colonists, is the American Revolution, which we commemorate at a time of extraordinary prosperity (p. 23, l. 1–p. 25, l. 14). A monument, it is true, cannot make the knowledge of these historical events more wide-spread, yet it can be of use in spreading love of country, in reminding all men of the principles of liberty (p. 25, l. 15–

p. 27, l. 17). Only fifty years from Bunker Hill we have seen marvelous changes both in this country and in Europe (p. 27, l. 18–p. 28, l. 33). While we are enjoying this unexampled prosperity, we have still among us survivors of the war; to you, survivors of Bunker Hill, to you also, unquenchable spirit (Warren), who gave up life on this field of war, and to you, veterans of half a century, we express our universal gratitude (p. 29, l. 1–p. 31, l. 31). Passing over the familiar incidents of the battle and the events leading up to it, we notice briefly that before the battle there was no strong feeling of unity in the colonies or abroad, but that after the battle all stood as a unit, shoulder to shoulder, against the mother country (p. 31, l. 32–p. 35, l. 14). To you, fortunate man (Lafayette), whom the news of these events roused to action, and through whom the electric spark of liberty was conducted from the New World to the Old, we express the happiness which your presence brings to us at this scene of commemoration of the deeds of the great patriots, and we express the hope that it may be long before anyone shall write your eulogy (p. 35, l. 15–p. 36, l. 26). Invited by the spirit of the occasion to consider the changes of the last fifty years in this country and elsewhere, we are impressed with three features that especially characterize the present age: (*a*) the vast spread of knowledge; (*b*) the improved condition of the individual; (*c*) the bettering effect of these two things on the state of the governments of the world (p. 36, l. 27–p. 43, l. 31). Our duty is to preserve unblemished to the world the cheering example of our popular government, and to hold sacred the obligations which have devolved on this generation (p. 43, l. 32–p. 45, l. 30).

From this analysis it will be seen that no one central theme is started at the beginning of the speech and developed systematically to the end. Instead, the orator takes up a number of items suggested by the nature of the occasion, and eloquently discusses each. Intermingled with these reflections are stirring apostrophes to the hero who was first celebrated by a monument on the battle site, to the heroes of the battle who were present in the audience, and to the distinguished guest from abroad. Yet it is evident that a single thought permeates the whole address, the thought of the duty of national patriotism, as an inheritance from those who made the nation possible. Surely in its general construction the speech measures up to the best tests of oratory of this character.

With regard to the details of the construction of the speech it may be pointed out that the individual paragraphs are excellent rhetorically and have also a genuine oratorical swing. Analyzed closely, most of the paragraphs will be found to contain a single idea developed thoroughly and consistently. Examine, for instance, the last paragraph of the oration, and observe how closely and energetically the speaker dwells on the idea of the duty of the men of 1825 in the carrying on of the free government established by their forefathers. The continuity of the thought, too, is admirable. From sentence to sentence the paragraph idea runs on to a forcible and effective final statement in the last sentence.

But the rhetorical analysis of the thought, revealing as it does, almost always, paragraph unity and continuity, scarcely reveals the spirited oratorical swing of the paragraphs. To feel this oratorical fervor is easier than to understand how it is gained, for there is always the element of emotion in utterances such as these. The gathering of groups of two or three or four similar phrases into a sentence, the repeating of the same form of sentence structure through a long series of sentences (see page 26), the modulation of effect by varying the sentence length, and the selection of strong Saxon words help in producing the oratorical tone. One can appreciate the speech fairly well through detailed examination of the paragraphs in order to discover these devices. Such a study is bound to reveal something of the secret of the orator, but from the very nature of

the address cannot be expected to bring one a complete understanding. This commemorative oration is pre-eminently one to
be felt and enjoyed through oral interpretation leading to an
increasing sense of the patriotic duties of the present generation. A genuine thrill of devotion to country roused by the
speech will be of more value than anything else to be gained
from its painstaking study, and will on the whole give one a
better conception of the true significance of the orator's effort
and its true place in the field of commemorative oratory.

Webster takes for granted a knowledge in his hearers of the
incidents of the battle. He says, on page 31, "The occasion
does not require of me any particular account of the battle
of the 17th of June, nor any detailed narrative of the events
which immediately preceded it." In the four following paragraphs, however, he does give a narrative of the events which
preceded the battle. He tells how Massachusetts had been
singled out by the English government as an object for severe
punishment, and he explains the effect upon that colony and
neighboring colonies of this severity of treatment. He points
out how the clash at Lexington and Concord accentuated the
bitter feeling of resistance and brought the united New England colonies to the next field of battle. So much, in brief,
he tells of the events preceding the battle.

Still, he neglects to give many incidents of the fight, assuming
a knowledge of these. Seven years before the time of his speech
he published, in the *North American Review* (July, 1818), a
glowing description of the Battle of Bunker Hill. Unfortunately most students nowadays do not seem to have the
knowledge which Webster takes for granted. Let us therefore start with the specific references which are made by the
speaker in his oration and then gather together a few other
items to give a connected idea of the contest. On page 29,
lines 9–16, Webster says to the venerable warriors, "You see
no mixed volumes of smoke and flame rising from burning

Charlestown. The ground strewed with the dead and the dying; the impetuous charge; the steady and successful repulse; the loud call to repeated assault; the summoning of all that is manly to repeated resistance; a thousand bosoms freely and fearlessly bared in an instant to whatever of terror may be in war and death; — all these you have witnessed, but you witness them no more." He then calls his venerable auditors' attention to the fact that the towers and roofs of Boston are now filled with the whole happy population, instead of with terrified wives and children, and to the fact that the ships in the Navy Yard at the base of the hill are the nation's, that they are not hostile sloops of war as on the day of the conflict. These details, it will be observed, are mostly oratorical generalizations; at most battles there is the impetuous charge and the summoning of manly courage to vigorous resistance. The only specific details are regarding the onlookers and the fleet, Again, there is a reference to the event on page 29, line 34, when the orator says that he looks in vain in the audience for Prescott, Putnam, Stark, Brooks, Read, Pomeroy, and Bridge, a great muster roll of names possessing for those who know the details of the battle something of the wonderful effect described by Macaulay as belonging to the catalogue of names in Milton's epic. Again, on page 36, lines 2–7, in the personal words to Lafayette, comes another reference, the most specific and definite contained in the speech. "You see the lines of the little redoubt thrown up by the incredible diligence of Prescott; defended, to the last extremity, by his lion-hearted valor; and within which the corner stone of our monument has now taken its position. You see where Warren fell, and where Parker, Gardner, McCleary, Moore, and other early patriots fell with him." Here, as before, the definiteness is largely that of a roll-call of honor, though the part taken by Prescott is mentioned specifically. The "little" redoubt, in a historical rather than an oratorical narrative, would be described as "eight rods square"

(Bancroft). With these three references, the details supplied by Webster stop. The account in his oration delivered 17 June, 1843, upon the completion of the monument, is also oratorical in its character, omitting specific historical details. Let us therefore go to Bancroft and Frothingham, the historians, for a connected, definite account of the contest.

The topography [1] of the battle ground is important to understand if one would grasp the essential facts of the contest. Richard Frothingham, in his centennial *Battle of Bunker Hill*, 1875, gives at page 15 an admirable diagram of the region. In the same author's pamphlet entitled *The Battle-field of Bunker Hill*, published in 1876, the frontispiece is an excellently clear engraving of early Charlestown. On a narrow peninsula north of Boston and separated from it by the Charles River, half a mile wide, was the village of Charlestown. The other side of the peninsula was bounded by the Mystic River. These elements in the situation are still about the same. There have been changes, however, in the hillsides, which, owing to the growth of Charlestown, do not retain their original contour. Just back of Charlestown was Breed's Hill, about seventy-five feet high. Beyond it, close to the neck of the peninsula, was a higher summit, Bunker Hill, a hundred and ten feet high. The ground sloped gradually down from Bunker Hill, then rose into Breed's Hill. It was difficult to tell just where one hill stopped and the other began. From Breed's Hill to the

---

[1] There is much confusion about the topography. Maps in popular histories differ widely. In the long list of nearly contemporary accounts, also, cited by Frothingham in his *History of the Siege of Boston*, there is much diversity of statement regarding the topographical features. Some of the accounts call the hill just back of Charlestown Bunker's Hill, and the one farther northwest, near the mouth of the peninsula, Breed's Hill; some call the hill back of the town Charlestown Hill. The map by a British officer appearing in Frothingham's History shows Bunker's Hill to have been directly back of Charlestown; but the account by the Committee of Safety, July 25, 1775, explicitly names the hill nearest the isthmus as Bunker Hill, and the one nearest Boston as Breed's Hill.

Charles River the descent was much sharper than it was on the other side. The two hills overlooked the whole region of Charlestown and Boston and the harbor. General Gage, leader of the British forces at Boston, planned to extend his fortifications to include these two strategic positions. The Massachusetts committee of safety determined to get ahead of the British commander. From this circumstance arose the Battle of Bunker Hill.

Colonel William Prescott, who volunteered for the work of fortification, was selected by the committee, and was put in command of a brigade of one thousand men. With an engineer named Grindley and this brigade, consisting of men of his own regiment and several detachments under Colonel Ebenezer Bridge, Major John Brooks, and other leaders, Prescott, provided with suitable intrenching tools, started silently on the evening of June 16 from Cambridge. They were raw soldiers, dressed in farmers' garb or the hunting-shirt of the frontiersman, volunteers armed mostly with fowling-pieces, without bayonets; men enlisted recently and coming from different Massachusetts and Connecticut regiments. The final instructions received were to fortify Breed's Hill, as being nearer Boston. Accordingly, it was there that Prescott and his men threw up a sod redoubt that night. It was on Breed's Hill that the brunt of the British attack fell; it was there that the most celebrated acts of valor were performed; and it is this hill, instead of Bunker Hill, that is now crowned by the monument. Prescott's work of fortification was not noticed by the British vessels at anchor in the Charles River. Next morning, however, the cannon of the British ship-of-war "Lively," which had lain unsuspectingly at anchor during the night in the ferry-way between Boston and Charlestown, opened fire on the redoubt. The people of Boston and the soldiers of England were alike puzzled by the unexpected appearance of a redoubt on Breed's Hill. A battery was soon bombarding the new redoubt from Copp's Hill, across the Charles River, in Boston. Some time after noon, more than two thousand British troops under Major General Howe and Brigadier General Pigot were transported to the north side of the peninsula, along which runs the Mystic River, to attack the colonial soldiers.

The news of the threatened attack brought reënforcements to Prescott, including Stark's and Reed's New Hampshire regiments, and a number of individuals who went on their own account, without orders, from Boston and Cambridge. Old General Seth Pomeroy was one of those who went from Boston; he was heartily cheered as he took his place with the rest, and he fought with the troops until the retreat, at the end animating the younger men with his shattered musket (Frothingham's *Battle of Bunker Hill*). Dr. Joseph Warren, president of Congress and provincial major general, was another, from Cambridge. In refusing to heed the entreaties of a friend who urged him to remain at home, Warren exclaimed, as we now know prophetically, *Dulce et decorum est pro patria mori*, "It is sweet and becoming to die for one's country" (*Life of Joseph Warren*, page 510, by Richard Frothingham). General Warren, whose "heroic soul elicited a kindred fire from the troops," was the last to leave the trenches when the colonists retreated from the redoubt on Breed's Hill, and he fell mortally wounded about sixty yards from the redoubt.

The contest which thus ended in retreat and the death of an intrepid and cultured volunteer, was fought with military precision by the veteran British soldiers and with patriotic stubbornness and valor by the colonists. The battery on Copp's Hill carried out Gage's threat made previously, and threw shells that set fire to the six hundred dwelling-houses, stores, and warehouses of Charlestown (G. W. Warren's *History of the Bunker Hill Monument Association*). Then the British forces, twenty-five hundred strong, which had landed on the Mystic side of the peninsula, began their advance. One column headed for the redoubt, the other for a harmless-looking rail fence stretching down from the redoubt toward the Mystic River. The fifteen hundred Americans were so placed on the peninsula in various positions — behind the rail fence, protected by a natural trench, on the summit of Bunker Hill, and in the Breed's Hill redoubt — that they were able to kill or wound a third of the forces opposed to them. At the order of Prescott and Putnam, in different parts of the battle field, the inexperienced colonial troops held their fire till the enemy were less than two hundred feet away, and sometimes less than sixty. The result of such deliberate and deadly firing was disastrous to the attacking force, which was twice repulsed. About four o'clock in the afternoon, after two hours of hot fighting, Prescott gave the order to retreat, himself parrying the bayonet strokes of oncoming veterans till his coat was slit in many places. Breaking through the enemy's attack promiscuously, most of the seven hundred who had been in the redoubt escaped, assisted in their retreat by the valiant soldiers at the rail fence who had twice repulsed the attacks from their side. Altogether, according to General Ward, one hundred and fifteen of the American soldiers were killed, and three hundred and five wounded; thirty were captured. Among the dead should be especially mentioned, besides Warren, Major Willard Moore, who was twice wounded, yet would not give up till his death; Thomas Gardner, of Cambridge, a member of Congress, killed by a random shot as he was descending Bunker Hill; Major Andrew McCleary, a brave, athletic New Hampshire farmer, six feet and a half tall, hit by a chance cannon ball at the isthmus joining the peninsula to the mainland; and Lieutenant Colonel Moses Parker, of Chelmsford, Massachusetts, who was wounded and taken prisoner, and who died in the Boston jail after the amputation of his leg. These details of the engagement will help to make plain Webster's references in his oration, so that further biographical or historical explanations may be dispensed with in the notes.

By the battle the British gained a place of encampment, but the colonists gained the sympathy and support of all the other colonists of America, and astonished their foes. The issue of *The Massachusetts Spy, or American Oracle of Liberty*, that appeared on June 21, 1775, concluded its account of the battle with the statement that though the scene was altogether new and horrible to the colonial volunteers, nevertheless they stood, many of them, and received numerous wounds before they quitted their lines; and four days after the battle they were all in high spirits. Franklin, impressed with this extraordinary showing of poorly equipped, ill-drilled patriots against veteran soldiers and celebrated generals, wrote confidently not long after the contest, "England has lost her colonies forever."

TOPICS AND QUESTIONS ON WASHINGTON'S ADDRESS

1. Some of the principal items that Hamilton felt ought to be included in the proposed address are:

(*a*) The Union as the rock of their salvation.

(*b*) Fitness of the parts of the Union for each other.

(*c*) The cherishing of the actual government.

(*d*) Morals, religion, industry, commerce, economy.

(*e*) The cherishing of good faith, justice, and peace with all other nations.

(*f*) A rule to have as little connection as possible with foreign nations.

Do these items include all the principal topics which Washington elaborated in his final form of the address?

2. Was the *Farewell Address* prepared to be spoken?

3. Does any part of the document seem eloquent?

4. To what extent does this state paper appear to you to reveal the character of Washington?

5. "The richest heritage that has come down to us from the Fathers of the Republic."

6. (*a*) In the notes on pages 1–9 is there any material that you knew already?

(*b*) Would you omit anything in the notes on these paragraphs if you were preparing annotative aids?

(*c*) Would you add anything?

7. Make a study of the sentence length in the address by actual count, finding in each paragraph how many sentences there are under thirty words in length compared with the number over thirty words in length.

8. (*a*) Do you consider the paragraphs mostly long or mostly short?

(*b*) What is your standard for length?

9. (*a*) Mention the principal propositions which Washington discusses, and reproduce his arguments on each proposition.

(*b*) Should you call the address mainly expository or mainly argumentative?

10. The salutation.

11. It has been said that the public addresses and state papers of Washington have much of the balancing of effects in the arrangement of series of clauses characteristic of the writings of Samuel Johnson, who was a model for many eighteenth-century authors. Where do you find in the *Farewell Address* any examples illustrating this characteristic?

12. Give Washington's expansion of three of the leading sentiments which he wished to impress upon the American people.

TOPICS AND QUESTIONS ON WEBSTER'S ORATION

1. Criticise the following topical outline of Webster's oration:

(*a*) Comparative importance of the event commemorated.

(*b*) Aim of the Society in building the monument.

(*c*) Abstract of happenings since the battle.

(*d*) Address to soldiers.

(*e*) The effect of the battle.

(*f*) Address to Lafayette.

(*g*) Character of the present age.

(*h*) Our duties as citizens of the foremost republican nation.

2. Make a detailed topical outline containing three main divisions: Introduction, Body, and Conclusion, and a number of further divisions under these main headings.

3. Give the substance of Webster's address to the soldiers of the war. [You will probably be able to tell this best if you will pretend for the time being that you are Webster and that you are speaking in the first person directly to the old soldiers.]

4. The object of the monument, as explained by Webster.

5. Show what the Battle of Bunker Hill accomplished.

6. Name and fully explain the figures of speech on page 39, lines 5–12.

7. Discuss page 43, line 32–page 44, line 9, with regard to unity and coherence.

8. Reproduce Webster's views on the relation of knowledge to liberty.

9. Show how the third sentence is necessary to the successful development of the central idea in the fourth paragraph.

10. Commit to memory the selection from Webster found on page xxxii.

11. Read the whole oration aloud, at one time or at different times, and make a record of how long it took you to read each main division. [The main divisions can easily be distinguished not only by the thought but by the extra space between these divisions. As readers use different rates of speed, the answers will probably differ widely.]

12. Prepare to speak an oratorical paragraph on some subject interesting to yourself and probably interesting to the rest of the class.

13. What impression did Webster make on American history?

14. As an orator, did Webster influence the speakers of his or any following generation to an appreciable degree?

15. Are the characteristics of true eloquence as explained by Webster to be found in his own *Bunker Hill Oration*?

16. Are there any touches of argumentation in Webster's address?

17. Using material found in this book or found by yourself elsewhere, write what would seem to you a satisfactory set of notes for pages 23–28.

18. Are the Washington and Webster addresses which appear in this volume literature?

BOOKS ON WASHINGTON AND WEBSTER

1. Biographies of Washington and Webster, by H. C. Lodge, in American Statesmen Series.

2. *The True George Washington*, by P. L. Ford.

3. *The Life of Daniel Webster*, by G. T. Curtis.

4. *The Writings of Washington*, edited by Jared Sparks and by W. C. Ford, and *The Works of Daniel Webster*, published by Little and Brown, 1851, and including a *Biographical Memoir* by Edward Everett.

WASHINGTON'S
FAREWELL ADDRESS

To the PEOPLE *of the* United States:

FRIENDS and FELLOW-CITIZENS,

1 THE period for a new election of a Citizen, to administer the executive government of the United States, being not far distant, and the time actually arrived, when your thoughts must be employed in designating the person, who is to be cloathed with that important trust, it appears to me proper, espe- 5 cially as it may conduce to a more distinct expression of the public voice, that I should now apprise you of the resolution I have formed, to decline being considered among the number of those, out of whom a choice is to be made.

2 I beg you, at the same time, to do me the justice to be 10 assured, that this resolution has not been taken, without a strict regard to all the considerations appertaining to the relation, which binds a dutiful citizen to his country; and that, in with-drawing the tender of service which silence in my situation might imply, I am influenced by no diminution of zeal for 15 your future interest; no deficiency of grateful respect for your past kindness; but am supported by a full conviction that the step is compatible with both.

3 The acceptance of, and continuance hitherto in the office to which your suffrages have twice called me, have been a 20 uniform sacrifice of inclination to the opinion of duty, and to a deference for what appeared to be your desire. I con-stantly hoped, that it would have been much earlier in my power, consistently with motives, which I was not at liberty to

disregard, to return to that retirement, from which I had been reluctantly drawn. The strength of my inclination to do this, previous to the last election, had even led to the preparation of an address to declare it to you; but mature reflection on
5 the then perplexed and critical posture of our affairs with foreign nations, and the unanimous advice of persons entitled to my confidence, impelled me to abandon the idea.

I rejoice, that the state of your concerns, external as well as internal, no longer renders the pursuit of inclination incom-
10 patible with the sentiment of duty, or propriety; and am persuaded whatever partiality may be retained for my services, that in the present circumstances of our country, you will not disapprove my determination to retire.

The impressions with which I first undertook the arduous
15 trust, were explained on the proper occasion. In the discharge of this trust, I will only say, that I have with good intentions, contributed towards the organization and administration of the government, the best exertions of which a very fallible judgment was capable. Not unconscious, in the out
20 set, of the inferiority of my qualifications, experience in my own eyes, perhaps still more in the eyes of others, has strengthened the motives to diffidence of myself; and every day the encreasing weight of years admonishes me more and more, that the shade of retirement is as necessary to me as it will be wel-
25 come. Satisfied that if any circumstances have given peculiar value to my services, they were temporary, I have the consolation to believe, that while choice and prudence invite me to quit the political scene, patriotism does not forbid it.

In looking forward to the moment, which is intended to
30 terminate the career of my public life, my feelings do not permit me to suspend the deep acknowledgment of that debt of gratitude which I owe to my beloved country, for the many honours it has conferred upon me; still more for the stedfast confidence with which it has supported me; and for

the opportunities I have thence enjoyed of manifesting my inviolable attachment, by services faithful and persevering, though in usefulness unequal to my zeal. If benefits have resulted to our country from these services, let it always be remembered to your praise, and as an instructive example in our annals, that under circumstances in which the passions, agitated in every direction, were liable to mislead, amidst appearances sometimes dubious, — vicissitudes of fortune often discouraging, — in situations in which not unfrequently want of success has countenanced the spirit of criticism — the constancy of your support was the essential prop of the efforts, and a guarantee of the plans by which they were effected. — Profoundly penetrated with this idea, I shall carry it with me to my grave, as a strong incitement to unceasing vows that Heaven may continue to you the choicest tokens of its beneficence — that your union and brotherly affection may be perpetual — that the free constitution, which is the work of your hands, may be sacredly maintained — that its administration in every department may be stamped with wisdom and virtue — that, in fine, the happiness of the people of these States, under the auspices of liberty, may be made complete, by so careful a preservation and so prudent a use of this blessing as will acquire to them the glory of recommending it to the applause, the affection and adoption of every nation which is yet a stranger to it.

Here, perhaps, I ought to stop. But a solicitude for your welfare, which cannot end but with my life, and the apprehension of danger, natural to that solicitude, urge me on an occasion like the present, to offer to your solemn contemplation, and to recommend to your frequent review, some sentiments, which are the result of much reflection, of no inconsiderable observation, and which appear to me all important to the permanency of your felicity as a People. These will be offered to you with the more freedom, as you can only see in them

the disinterested warnings of a parting friend, who can possibly
have no personal motive to bias his counsel. Nor can I forget, as an encouragement to it, your indulgent reception of my
sentiments on a former and not dissimilar occasion.

5 § Interwoven as is the love of liberty with every ligament of
your hearts, no recommendation of mine is necessary to fortify
or confirm the attachment.

9 The Unity of Government which constitutes you one people, is also now dear to you. It is justly so; for it is a main
10 pillar in the edifice of your real independence, the support of
your tranquility at home, your peace abroad; of your safety;
of your prosperity; of that very Liberty which you so highly
prize. But as it is easy to foresee, that from different causes
and from different quarters, much pains will be taken, many
15 artifices employed, to weaken in your minds the conviction of
this truth; as this is the point in your political fortress against
which the batteries of internal and external enemies will be
most constantly and actively (though often covertly and insidi-
ously) directed, it is of infinite moment, that you should
20 properly estimate the immense value of your national Union,
to your collective and individual happiness; that you should
cherish a cordial, habitual and immoveable attachment to it;
accustoming yourselves to think and speak of it as of the
Palladium of your political safety and prosperity; watching for
25 its preservation with jealous anxiety; discountenancing whatever may suggest even a suspicion that it can in any event be
abandoned; and indignantly frowning upon the first dawning
of every attempt to alienate any portion of our country from
the rest, or to enfeeble the sacred ties which now link together
30 the various parts.

10 For this you have every inducement of sympathy and interest. Citizens by birth or choice, of a common country,
that country has a right to concentrate your affections. The
name of AMERICAN, which belongs to you, in your national

capacity, must always exalt the just pride of Patriotism, more than any appellation derived from local discriminations. With slight shades of difference, you have the same religion, manners, habits and political principles. You have in a common cause fought and triumphed together; the Independence and Liberty you possess are the work of joint councils, and joint efforts, of common dangers, sufferings and successes.

But these considerations, however powerfully they address themselves to your sensibility, are greatly outweighed by those which apply more immediately to your interest. — Here every portion of our country finds the most commanding motives for carefully guarding and preserving the Union of the whole.

The *North*, in an unrestrained intercourse with the *South*, protected by the equal laws of a common government, finds in the productions of the latter, great additional resources of maritime and commercial enterprise and precious materials of manufacturing industry. — The *South* in the same intercourse, benefitting by the Agency of the *North*, sees its agriculture grow and its commerce expand. Turning partly into its own channels the seamen of the *North*, it finds its particular navigation invigorated; — and while it contributes, in different ways, to nourish and increase the general mass of the national navigation, it looks forward to the protection of a maritime strength, to which itself is unequally adapted. — The *East*, in a like intercourse with the *West*, already finds, and in the progressive improvement of interior communications, by land and water, will more and more find a valuable vent for the commodities which it brings from abroad, or manufactures at home. — The *West* derives from the *East* supplies requisite to its growth and comfort — and what is perhaps of still greater consequence, it must of necessity owe the *secure* enjoyment of indispensable *outlets* for its own productions to the weight, influence, and the future maritime strength of the Atlantic side of the Union, directed by an indissoluble community of interest as *one nation.* — Any other tenure by which the *West* can hold this essential advantage, whether derived from its own separate strength, or from an apostate and unnatural connection with any foreign power, must be intrinsically precarious.

5 13 While then every part of our country thus feels an immediate and particular interest in Union, all the parts combined cannot fail to find in the united mass of means and efforts greater strength, greater resource, proportionably greater security from external danger, a less frequent interruption of
10 their peace by foreign nations ; — and what is of inestimable value ! they must derive from Union an exemption from those broils and wars between themselves, which so frequently afflict neighbouring countries, not tied together by the same government ; which their own rivalships alone would be suffi-
15 cient to produce, but which opposite foreign alliances, attachments and intrigues would stimulate and imbitter. — Hence likewise they will avoid the necessity of those overgrown military establishments, which under any form of government are inauspicious to liberty, and which are to be regarded as par-
20 ticularly hostile to Republican Liberty.   In this sense it is, that your Union ought to be considered as a main prop of your liberty, and that the love of the one ought to endear to you the preservation of the other.

14 These considerations speak a persuasive language to every
25 reflecting and virtuous mind, and exhibit the continuance of the UNION as a primary object of Patriotic desire. — Is there a doubt, whether a common government can embrace so large a sphere ? — Let experience solve it.   To listen to mere speculation in such a case were criminal.   We are authorized to hope
30 that a proper organization of the whole, with the auxiliary agency of governments for the respective subdivisions, will afford a happy issue to the experiment.   'T is well worth a fair and full experiment.   With such powerful and obvious motives to Union, affecting all parts of our country, while

experience shall not have demonstrated its impracticability, there will always be reason to distrust the patriotism of those, who in any quarter may endeavour to weaken its bands.

5 In contemplating the causes which may disturb our Union, it occurs as matter of serious concern, that any ground should have been furnished for characterising parties by *Geographical* discriminations — *Northern* and *Southern* — *Atlantic* and *Western;* whence designing men may endeavour to excite a belief that there is a real difference of local interests and views. One of the expedients of party to acquire influence, within particular districts, is to misrepresent the opinions and aims of other districts. You cannot shield yourselves too much against the jealousies and heart burnings which spring from these misrepresentations: they tend to render alien to each other those who ought to be bound together by fraternal affection. The inhabitants of our western country have lately had a useful lesson on this head: they have seen, in the negociation by the Executive, and in the unanimous ratification by the Senate, of the treaty with Spain, and in the universal satisfaction at that event, throughout the United States, a decisive proof how unfounded were the suspicions propagated among them of a policy in the General Government and in the Atlantic States unfriendly to their interests in regard to the MISSISSIPPI: they have been witnesses to the formation of two treaties, that with Great Britain and that with Spain, which secure to them every thing they could desire, in respect to our foreign relations, towards confirming their prosperity. Will it not be their wisdom to rely for the preservation of these advantages on the UNION by which they were procured? Will they not henceforth be deaf to those advisers, if such there are, who would sever them from their Brethren and connect them with aliens?

6 To the efficacy and permanency of your Union, a government for the whole is indispensable. — No alliances, however strict, between the parts can be an adequate substitute; they

must inevitably experience the infractions and interruptions which all alliances in all times have experienced. Sensible of this momentous truth, you have improved upon your first essay, by the adoption of a Constitution of Government better
5 calculated than your former for an intimate Union, and for the efficacious management of your common concerns. This Government, the offspring of our own choice, uninfluenced and unawed, adopted upon full investigation and mature delibera- tion, completely free in its principles, in the distribution of its
10 powers, uniting security with energy, and containing within itself a provision for its own amendment, has a just claim to your confidence and your support. Respect for its authority, compliance with its laws, acquiescence in its measures, are duties enjoined by the fundamental maxims of true Liberty.
15 The basis of our political systems is the right of the people to make and to alter their Constitutions of Government. — But, the Constitution which at any time exists, 'till changed by an explicit and authentic act of the whole people, is sacredly ob- ligatory upon all. The very idea of the power and the right
20 of the people to establish government presupposes the duty of every individual to obey the established Government.

¶ All obstructions to the execution of the Laws, all combi- nations and associations, under whatever plausible character, with the real design to direct, controul, counteract, or awe the
25 regular deliberation and action of the constituted authorities, are destructive of this fundamental principle, and of fatal tendency. They serve to organize faction, to give it an arti- ficial and extraordinary force — to put in the place of the dele- gated will of the nation, the will of a party, often a small but
30 artful and enterprizing minority of the community; and, ac- cording to the alternate triumphs of different parties, to make the public administration the mirror of the ill concerted and incongruous projects of faction, rather than the organ of con- sistent and wholesome plans digested by common councils, and

modified by mutual interests. However combinations or associations of the above description may now and then answer
popular ends, they are likely in the course of time and things
to become potent engines, by which cunning, ambitious and
unprincipled men will be enabled to subvert the power of the 5
people, and to usurp for themselves the reins of government;
destroying afterwards the very engines which have lifted them
to unjust dominion.

Towards the preservation of your government, and the permanency of your present happy state, it is requisite, not only 10
that you speedily discountenance irregular oppositions to its
acknowledged authority, but also that you resist with care the
spirit of innovation upon its principles however specious the
pretexts.—One method of assault may be to effect in the forms
of the constitution alterations which will impair the energy of 15
the system, and thus to undermine what cannot be directly
overthrown.   In all the changes to which you may be invited,
remember that time and habit are at least as necessary to fix
the true character of governments, as of other human institutions — that experience is the surest standard, by which to test 20
the real tendency of the existing constitution of a country —
that facility in changes upon the credit of mere hypothesis and
opinion, exposes to perpetual change, from the endless variety
of hypothesis and opinion ; and remember, especially, that for
the efficient management of your common interests, in a 25
country so extensive as ours, a government of as much vigour
as is consistent with the perfect security of liberty, is indispensable.   Liberty itself will find in such a government, with powers
properly distributed and adjusted, its surest guardian.   It is,
indeed, little else than a name, where the government is too 30
feeble to withstand the enterprises of faction, to confine each
member of the society within the limits prescribed by the laws,
and to maintain all in the secure and tranquil enjoyment of the
rights of person and property.

19   I have already intimated to you, the danger of parties in the state, with particular reference to the founding of them on geographical discriminations. Let me now take a more comprehensive view, and warn you in the most solemn 5 manner against the baneful effects of the spirit of party, generally.

20   This spirit, unfortunately, is inseparable from our nature, having its root in the strongest passions of the human mind.— It exists under different shapes in all governments, more or less 10 stifled, controuled, or repressed; but in those of the popular form, it is seen in its greatest rankness and is truly their worst enemy.

21   The alternate domination of one faction over another, sharpened by the spirit of revenge, natural to party dissention, 15 which in different ages and countries has perpetrated the most horrid enormities, is itself a frightful despotism.— But this leads at length to a more formal and permanent despotism.— The disorders and miseries, which result, gradually incline the minds of men to seek security and repose in the absolute power of an 20 individual: and sooner or later the chief of some prevailing faction more able or more fortunate than his competitors, turns this disposition to the purposes of his own elevation, on the ruins of Public Liberty.

22   Without looking forward to an extremity of this kind (which 25 nevertheless ought not to be entirely out of sight) the common and continual mischiefs of the spirit of party are sufficient to make it the interest and duty of a wise People to discourage and restrain it.

23   It serves always to distract the Public Councils and enfeeble 30 the Public Administration. It agitates the Community with ill founded jealousies and false alarms; kindles the animosity of one part against another, foments occasionally riot and insurrection. It opens the door to foreign influence and corruption, which find a facilitated access to the government itself

through the channels of party passions.   Thus the policy and
the will of one country are subjected to the policy and will of
another.

24   There is an opinion that parties in free countries are useful
checks upon the administration of the Government, and serve 5
to keep alive the spirit of Liberty.   This within certain limits
is probably true ; and in Governments of a Monarchical cast,
Patriotism may look with indulgence, if not with favour upon
the spirit of party.   But in those of the popular character, in
Governments purely elective, it is a spirit not to be encouraged. 10
From their natural tendency, it is certain there will always be
enough of that spirit for every salutary purpose.   And there
being constant danger of excess, the effort ought to be, by force
of public opinion, to mitigate and assuage it.   A fire not to be
quenched ; it demands a uniform vigilance to prevent its burst- 15
ing into flame, lest, instead of warming it should consume.

25   It is important likewise, that the habits of thinking in a free
country, should inspire caution, in those entrusted with its
administration, to confine themselves within their respective
constitutional spheres, avoiding in the exercise of the powers 20
of one department to encroach upon another.   The spirit of
encroachment tends to consolidate the powers of all the departments in one, and thus to create, whatever the form of government, a real despotism.   A just estimate of that love of power,
and proneness to abuse it, which predominates in the human 25
heart, is sufficient to satisfy us of the truth of this position.
The necessity of reciprocal checks in the exercise of political
power ; by dividing and distributing it into different deposito-
ries, and constituting each the Guardian of the Public Weal
against invasions by the others, has been evinced by experi- 30
ments ancient and modern : some of them in our country and
under our own eyes.   To preserve them must be as necessary
as to institute them.   If, in the opinion of the People, the distribution or modification of the constitutional powers be in

any particular wrong, let it be corrected by an amendment in the way which the constitution designates. — But let there be no change by usurpation ; for though this, in one instance, may be the instrument of good, it is the customary weapon by
5 which free governments are destroyed. — The precedent must always greatly overbalance in permanent evil any partial or transient benefit which the use can at any time yield.

Of all the dispositions and habits which lead to political prosperity, Religion and Morality are indispensable supports.
10 — In vain would that man claim the tribute of Patriotism, who should labour to subvert these great pillars of human happiness, these firmest props of the duties of Men and Citizens. — The mere Politician, equally with the pious man ought to respect and to cherish them. — A volume could not trace
15 all their connections with private and public felicity. Let it simply be asked where is the security for property, for reputation, for life, if the sense of religious obligation *desert* the oaths, which are the instruments of investigation in Courts of Justice ? And let us with caution indulge the supposition,
20 that morality can be maintained without religion. Whatever may be conceded to the influence of refined education on minds of peculiar structure ; reason and experience both forbid us to expect that national morality can prevail in exclusion of religious principle.

25 'T is substantially true, that virtue or morality is a necessary spring of popular government. The rule indeed extends with more or less force to every species of free government. Who that is a sincere friend to it can look with indifference upon attempts to shake the foundation of the fabric?

30 Promote, then, as an object of primary importance, institutions for the general diffusion of knowledge. — In proportion as the structure of a government gives force to public opinion, it is essential that public opinion should be enlightened.

As a very important source of strength and security cherish

public credit. One method of preserving it is to use it as sparingly as possible ; avoiding occasions of expence by cultivating peace, but remembering also that timely disbursements to prepare for danger frequently prevent much greater disbursements to repel it ; avoiding likewise the accumulation of debt, not only by shunning occasions of expence, but by vigorous exertions in time of peace to discharge the debts which unavoidable wars may have occasioned, not ungenerously throwing upon posterity the burthen which we ourselves ought to bear. — The execution of these maxims belongs to your representatives, but it is necessary that public opinion should co-operate. — To facilitate to them the performance of their duty, it is essential that you should practically bear in mind, that towards the payment of debts there must be Revenue ; that to have Revenue there must be taxes ; that no taxes can be devised which are not more or less inconvenient and unpleasant ; that the intrinsic embarrassment inseparable from the selection of the proper objects (which is always a choice of difficulties) ought to be a decisive motive for a candid construction of the conduct of the government in making it, and for a spirit of acquiescence in the measures for obtaining Revenue which the public exigencies may at any time dictate.

Observe good faith and justice towards all Nations, cultivate peace and harmony with all ; Religion and Morality enjoin this conduct ; and can it be that good policy does not equally enjoin it ? It will be worthy of a free, enlightened, and, at no distant period, a great Nation, to give to mankind the magnanimous and too novel example of a people always guided by an exalted justice and benevolence. Who can doubt that in the course of time and things the fruits of such a plan would richly repay any temporary advantages which might be lost by a steady adherence to it ? Can it be, that Providence has not connected the permanent felicity of a Nation with its Virtue ? The experiment, at least, is recommended by every sentiment which ennobles human nature.   Alas! is it rendered impossible by its vices?

31   In the execution of such a plan, nothing is more essential than that permanent, inveterate antipathies against particular Nations, and passionate attachments for others should be excluded; and that in place of them just and amicable feelings towards all should be cultivated.   The Nation, which indulges towards another an habitual hatred, or an habitual fondness, is in some degree a slave.   It is a slave to its animosity or to its affection, either of which is sufficient to lead it astray from its duty and its interest.   Antipathy in one nation against another disposes each more readily to offer insult and injury, to lay hold of slight causes of umbrage, and to be haughty and intractable, when accidental or trifling occasions of dispute occur.   Hence frequent collisions, obstinate, envenomed and bloody contests. The Nation, prompted by ill will and resentment, sometimes impels to war the Government, contrary to the best calculations of policy.   The Government sometimes participates in the national propensity, and adopts through passion what reason would reject; at other times, it makes the animosity of the nation subservient to projects of hostility instigated by pride, ambition and other sinister and pernicious motives. The peace often, sometimes perhaps the liberty, of Nations has been the victim.

32 So likewise, a passionate attachment of one Nation for another produces a variety of evils.   Sympathy for the favourite Nation, facilitating the illusion of an imaginary common interest, in cases where no real common interest exists, and infusing into one the enmities of the other, betrays the former into a participation in the quarrels and wars of the latter, without adequate inducement or justification.   It leads also to concessions to the favourite Nation of privileges denied to others, which is apt doubly to injure the Nation making the concessions; by unnecessarily parting with what ought to have been

retained ; and by exciting jealousy, ill will, and a disposition to retaliate, in the parties from whom equal privileges are with-held. And it gives to ambitious, corrupted, or deluded citizens (who devote themselves to the favourite nation) facility to betray, or sacrifice the interests of their own country, without 5 odium, sometimes even with popularity ; gilding with the appearances of a virtuous sense of obligation, a commendable deference for public opinion, or a laudable zeal for public good, the base or foolish compliances of ambition, corruption or infatuation. 10

As avenues to foreign influence in innumerable ways, such attachments are particularly alarming to the truly enlightened and independent Patriot. How many opportunities do they afford to tamper with domestic factions, to practice the arts of seduction, to mislead public opinion, to influence or awe the 15 Public Councils ! Such an attachment of a small or weak, towards a great and powerful nation, dooms the former to be the satellite of the latter.

Against the insidious wiles of foreign influence (I conjure you to believe me, fellow-citizens) the jealousy of a free people 20 ought to be *constantly* awake ; since history and experience prove that foreign influence is one of the most baneful foes of Republican Government. But that jealousy to be useful must be impartial ; else it becomes the instrument of the very influ-ence to be avoided, instead of a defence against it. — Ex- 25 cessive partiality for one foreign nation, and excessive dislike of another, cause those whom they actuate to see danger only on one side, and serve to veil and even second the arts of influence on the other. — Real patriots, who may resist the intrigues of the favourite, are liable to become suspected and 30 odious ; while its tools and dupes usurp the applause and con-fidence of the people, to surrender their interests.

The great rule of conduct for us, in regard to foreign na-tions, is in extending our commercial relations, to have with

them as little *political* connection as possible. So far as we
have already formed engagements, let them be fulfilled with
perfect good faith. — Here let us stop.

36 Europe has a set of primary interests, which to us have none,
or a very remote relation. Hence she must be engaged in
frequent controversies, the causes of which are essentially
foreign to our concerns. Hence, therefore, it must be unwise
in us to implicate ourselves, by artificial ties, in the ordinary
vicissitudes of her politics, or the ordinary combinations and
collisions of her friendships, or enmities.

37 Our detached and distant situation invites and enables us to
pursue a different course. If we remain one people, under an
efficient government, the period is not far off, when we may
defy material injury from external annoyance; when we may
take such an attitude as will cause the neutrality, we may at
any time resolve upon, to be scrupulously respected; when
belligerent nations, under the impossibility of making acqui-
sitions upon us, will not lightly hazard the giving us provoca-
tion; when we may choose peace or war, as our interest,
guided by justice, shall counsel.

38 Why forego the advantages of so peculiar a situation? Why
quit our own to stand upon foreign ground? Why, by inter-
weaving our destiny with that of any part of Europe, entangle
our peace and prosperity in the toils of European ambition,
rivalship, interest, humour or caprice?

39 'T is our true policy to steer clear of permanent alliances,
with any portion of the foreign world; so far, I mean, as we
are now at liberty to do it; for let me not be understood as
capable of patronising infidelity to existing engagements. I
hold the maxim no less applicable to public than to private
affairs, that honesty is always the best policy. I repeat it,
therefore, let those engagements be observed in their genuine
sense. But in my opinion, it is unnecessary and would be
unwise to extend them.

40 Taking care always to keep ourselves, by suitable establishments, on a respectable defensive posture, we may safely trust to temporary alliances for extraordinary emergencies.

41 Harmony, liberal intercourse with all nations, are recommended by policy, humanity, and interest. But even cur 5 commercial policy should hold an equal and impartial hand; neither seeking nor granting exclusive favours or preferences; consulting the natural course of things; diffusing and diversifying by gentle means the streams of commerce, but forcing nothing; establishing, with powers so disposed — in order to 10 give trade a stable course, to define the rights of our merchants, and to enable the government to support them — conventional rules of intercourse, the best that present circumstances and mutual opinion will permit, but temporary, and liable to be from time to time abandoned or varied, as experi- 15 ence and circumstances shall dictate; constantly keeping in view, that 't is folly in one nation to look for disinterested favours from another; that it must pay with a portion of its independence for whatever it may accept under that character; that by such acceptance, it may place itself in the condi- 20 tion of having given equivalents for nominal favours, and yet of being reproached with ingratitude for not giving more. There can be no greater error than to expect, or calculate upon real favours from nation to nation. 'T is an illusion which experience must cure, which a just pride ought to discard. 25

42 In offering to you, my countrymen, these counsels of an old and affectionate friend, I dare not hope they will make the strong and lasting impression I could wish; that they will controul the usual current of the passions, or prevent our nation from running the course which has hitherto marked the 30 destiny of nations. But if I may even flatter myself, that they may be productive of some partial benefit, some occasional good; that they may now and then recur to moderate the

fury of party spirit, to warn against the mischiefs of foreign
intrigue, to guard against the impostures of pretended patriotism ; this hope will be a full recompence for the solicitude for
your welfare, by which they have been dictated.

5 43 How far in the discharge of my official duties, I have been
guided by the principles which have been delineated, the public records and other evidences of my conduct must witness
to you and to the world.   To myself, the assurance of my own
conscience is, that I have at least believed myself to be guided
10 by them.

44 In relation to the still subsisting war in Europe, my Proclamation of the 22nd of April 1793 is the index to my Plan.
Sanctioned by your approving voice and by that of your
Representatives in both Houses of Congress, the spirit of that
15 measure has continually governed me ; uninfluenced by any
attempts to deter or divert me from it.

45 After deliberate examination with the aid of the best lights I
could obtain, I was well satisfied that our country, under all
the circumstances of the case, had a right to take, and was
20 bound in duty and interest, to take a neutral position.   Having taken it, I determined, as far as should depend upon me,
to maintain it, with moderation, perseverance and firmness.

46 The considerations which respect the right to hold this
conduct, it is not necessary on this occasion to detail.   I
25 will only observe, that according to my understanding of the
matter, that right, so far from being denied by any of the
Belligerent Powers, has been virtually admitted by all.

47 The duty of holding a neutral conduct may be inferred,
without any thing more, from the obligation which justice and
30 humanity impose on every nation, in cases in which it is free
to act, to maintain inviolate the relations of peace and amity
towards other nations.

48 The inducements of interest for observing that conduct will
best be referred to your own reflections and experience.   With

me, a predominant motive has been to endeavour to gain time to our country to settle and mature its yet recent institutions, and to progress without interruption, to that degree of strength and consistency, which is necessary to give it, humanly speaking, the command of its own fortunes. 5

Though in reviewing the incidents of my administration, I am unconscious of intentional error : I am nevertheless too sensible of my defects not to think it probable that I may have committed many errors. Whatever they may be I fervently beseech the Almighty to avert or mitigate the evils to 10 which they may tend. I shall also carry with me the hope that my Country will never cease to view them with indulgence ; and that after forty-five years of my life dedicated to its service, with an upright zeal, the faults of incompetent abilities will be consigned to oblivion, as myself must soon be 15 to the mansions of rest.

Relying on its kindness in this as in other things, and actuated by that fervent love towards it, which is so natural to a man, who views in it the native soil of himself and his progenitors for several generations ; I anticipate with pleasing 20 expectation that retreat, in which I promise myself to realize, without alloy, the sweet enjoyment of partaking, in the midst of my fellow citizens, the benign influence of good laws under a free government — the ever favourite object of my heart, and the happy reward, as I trust, of our mutual cares, labours 25 and dangers.

G. WASHINGTON.

United States, 17th September, 1796.

Topics of paragraphs,

AN

ADDRESS

DELIVERED AT THE LAYING OF THE

Corner Stone

OF THE

BUNKER HILL MONUMENT.

BY DANIEL WEBSTER.

BOSTON:

PUBLISHED BY CUMMINGS, HILLIARD, AND COMPANY

1825.

DANIEL WEBSTER

(After a daguerreotype)

WEBSTER'S
FIRST BUNKER HILL ORATION

THIS uncounted multitude before me, and around me, proves the feeling which the occasion has excited. These thousands of human faces, glowing with sympathy and joy, and, from the impulses of a common gratitude, turned reverently to heaven, in this spacious temple of the firmament, proclaim that the day, 5 the place, and the purpose of our assembling have made a deep impression on our hearts.

If, indeed, there be any thing in local association fit to affect the mind of man, we need not strive to repress the emotions which agitate us here. We are among the sepulchres of 10 our fathers. We are on ground, distinguished by their valor, their constancy, and the shedding of their blood. We are here, not to fix an uncertain date in our annals, nor to draw into notice an obscure and unknown spot. If our humble purpose had never been conceived, if we ourselves had never been 15 born, the 17th of June 1775 would have been a day on which all subsequent history would have poured its light, and the eminence where we stand, a point of attraction to the eyes of successive generations. But we are Americans. We live in what

NOTE. — As the pupil reads the oration through for the first time to get the author's meaning, he should, if he owns his copy, underline the words or expressions the meanings of which are not clear to him. Then, after finishing the reading of a lesson, he should look at the notes in the back of the book to see if the editor has anticipated his difficulty. The items which still seem obscure should then be looked up in any available reference books. In this way the reader will have the satisfaction of working out just what the speaker means.

may be called the early age of this great continent; and we
know that our posterity, through all time, are here to suffer
and enjoy the allotments of humanity. We see before us a
probable train of great events; we know that our own fortunes
5 have been happily cast; and it is natural, therefore, that we
should be moved by the contemplation of occurrences which
have guided our destiny before many of us were born, and
settled the condition in which we should pass that portion of
our existence, which God allows to men on earth.

10 We do not read even of the discovery of this continent,
without feeling something of a personal interest in the event;
without being reminded how much it has affected our own fortunes, and our own existence. It is more impossible for us,
therefore, than for others, to contemplate with unaffected minds
15 that interesting, I may say, that most touching and pathetic
scene, when the great Discoverer of America stood on the deck
of his shattered bark, the shades of night falling on the sea, yet
no man sleeping; tossed on the billows of an unknown ocean,
yet the stronger billows of alternate hope and despair tossing
20 his own troubled thoughts; extending forward his harassed
frame, straining westward his anxious and eager eyes, till
Heaven at last granted him a moment of rapture and ecstacy,
in blessing his vision with the sight of the unknown world.

Nearer to our times, more closely connected with our fates,
25 and therefore still more interesting to our feelings and affections,
is the settlement of our own country by colonists from England. We cherish every memorial of these worthy ancestors; we
celebrate their patience and fortitude; we admire their daring
enterprise; we teach our children to venerate their piety; and
30 we are justly proud of being descended from men, who have
set the world an example of founding civil institutions on the
great and united principles of human freedom and human
knowledge. To us, their children, the story of their labors
and sufferings can never be without its interest. We shall not

stand unmoved on the shore of Plymouth, while the sea continues to wash it; nor will our brethren in another early and ancient colony, forget the place of its first establishment, till their river shall cease to flow by it. No vigor of youth, no maturity of manhood, will lead the nation to forget the spots where its infancy was cradled and defended.

But the great event, in the history of the continent, which we are now met here to commemorate; that prodigy of modern times, at once the wonder and the blessing of the world, is the American Revolution. In a day of extraordinary prosperity and happiness, of high national honor, distinction, and power, we are brought together, in this place, by our love of country, by our admiration of exalted character, by our gratitude for signal services and patriotic devotion.

The society, whose organ I am, was formed for the purpose of rearing some honorable and durable monument to the memory of the early friends of American Independence. They have thought, that for this object no time could be more propitious, than the present prosperous and peaceful period; that no place could claim preference over this memorable spot; and that no day could be more auspicious to the undertaking, than the anniversary of the battle which was here fought. The foundation of that monument we have now laid. With solemnities suited to the occasion, with prayers to Almighty God for his blessing, and in the midst of this cloud of witnesses, we have begun the work. We trust it will be prosecuted; and that springing from a broad foundation, rising high in massive solidity and unadorned grandeur, it may remain, as long as Heaven permits the works of man to last, a fit emblem, both of the events in memory of which it is raised, and of the gratitude of those who have reared it.

We know, indeed, that the record of illustrious actions is most safely deposited in the universal remembrance of man-

kind. We know, that if we could cause this structure to
ascend, not only till it reached the skies, but till it pierced
them, its broad surfaces could still contain but part of that,
which, in an age of knowledge, hath already been spread over
5 the earth, and which history charges itself with making known
to all future times. We know, that no inscription on entablatures less broad than the earth itself, can carry information of
the events we commemorate, where it has not already gone ;
and that no structure, which shall not outlive the duration of
10 letters and knowledge among men, can prolong the memorial.
But our object is, by this edifice to show our own deep sense
of the value and importance of the achievements of our ancestors ; and, by presenting this work of gratitude to the eye, to
keep alive similar sentiments, and to foster a constant regard
15 for the principles of the Revolution. Human beings are composed not of reason only, but of imagination also, and sentiment ; and that is neither wasted nor misapplied which is
appropriated to the purpose of giving right direction to sentiments, and opening proper springs of feeling in the heart.
20 Let it not be supposed that our object is to perpetuate national
hostility, or even to cherish a mere military spirit. It is higher,
purer, nobler. We consecrate our work to the spirit of national independence, and we wish that the light of peace may
rest upon it forever. We rear a memorial of our conviction of
25 that unmeasured benefit, which has been conferred on our own
land, and of the happy influences, which have been produced,
by the same events, on the general interests of mankind. We
come, as Americans, to mark a spot, which must forever be
dear to us and our posterity. We wish, that whosoever, in all
30 coming time, shall turn his eye hither, may behold that the
place is not undistinguished, where the first great battle of
the Revolution was fought. We wish, that this structure may
proclaim the magnitude and importance of that event, to every
class and every age. We wish, that infancy may learn the

purpose of its erection from maternal lips, and that weary and withered age may behold it, and be solaced by the recollections which it suggests. We wish, that labor may look up here, and be proud, in the midst of its toil. We wish, that, in those days of disaster, which, as they come on all nations, must be expected to come on us also, desponding patriotism may turn its eyes hitherward, and be assured that the foundations of our national power still stand strong. We wish, that this column, rising towards heaven among the pointed spires of so many temples dedicated to God, may contribute also to produce, in all minds, a pious feeling of dependence and gratitude. We wish, finally, that the last object on the sight of him who leaves his native shore, and the first to gladden his who revisits it, may be something which shall remind him of the liberty and the glory of his country. Let it rise, till it meet the sun in his coming; let the earliest light of the morning gild it, and parting day linger and play on its summit.

We live in a most extraordinary age. Events so various and so important, that they might crowd and distinguish centuries, are, in our times, compressed within the compass of a single life. When has it happened that history has had so much to record, in the same term of years, as since the 17th of June 1775? Our own Revolution, which, under other circumstances, might itself have been expected to occasion a war of half a century, has been achieved; twenty-four sovereign and independent states erected; and a general government established over them, so safe, so wise, so free, so practical, that we might well wonder its establishment should have been accomplished so soon, were it not far the greater wonder that it should have been established at all. Two or three millions of people have been augmented to twelve; and the great forests of the West prostrated beneath the arm of successful industry; and the dwellers on the banks of the Ohio

and the Mississippi, become the fellow citizens and neighbours of those who cultivate the hills of New England. We
have a commerce, that leaves no sea unexplored ; navies,
which take no law from superior force ; revenues, adequate
5 to all the exigencies of government, almost without taxation ;
and peace with all nations, founded on equal rights and mutual
respect.

Europe, within the same period, has been agitated by a
mighty revolution, which, while it has been felt in the individ-
10 ual condition and happiness of almost every man, has shaken
to the centre her political fabric, and dashed against one
another thrones, which had stood tranquil for ages. On this,
our continent, our own example has been followed ; and colonies have sprung up to be nations. Unaccustomed sounds of
15 liberty and free government have reached us from beyond the
track of the sun ; and at this moment the dominion of European power, in this continent, from the place where we stand
to the south pole, is annihilated forever.

In the mean time, both in Europe and America, such has
20 been the general progress of knowledge ; such the improvements in legislation, in commerce, in the arts, in letters, and
above all in liberal ideas, and the general spirit of the age,
that the whole world seems changed.

Yet, notwithstanding that this is but a faint abstract of the
25 things which have happened since the day of the battle of
Bunker Hill, we are but fifty years removed from it ; and we
now stand here, to enjoy all the blessings of our own condition, and to look abroad on the brightened prospects of the
world, while we hold still among us some of those, who were
30 active agents in the scenes of 1775, and who are now here, from
every quarter of New England, to visit, once more, and under
circumstances so affecting, I had almost said so overwhelming,
this renowned theatre of their courage and patriotism.

VENERABLE MEN! you have come down to us, from a former generation. Heaven has bounteously lengthened out your lives, that you might behold this joyous day. You are now, where you stood, fifty years ago, this very hour, with your brothers, and your neighbours, shoulder to shoulder, in the strife for your country. Behold, how altered! The same heavens are indeed over your heads; the same ocean rolls at your feet; but all else, how changed! You hear now no roar of hostile cannon, you see no mixed volumes of smoke and flame rising from burning Charlestown. The ground strewed with the dead and the dying; the impetuous charge; the steady and successful repulse; the loud call to repeated assault; the summoning of all that is manly to repeated resistance; a thousand bosoms freely and fearlessly bared in an instant to whatever of terror there may be in war and death; — all these you have witnessed, but you witness them no more. All is peace. The heights of yonder metropolis, its towers and roofs, which you then saw filled with wives and children and countrymen in distress and terror, and looking with unutterable emotions for the issue of the combat, have presented you to-day with the sight of its whole happy population, come out to welcome and greet you with an universal jubilee. Yonder proud ships, by a felicity of position appropriately lying at the foot of this mount, and seeming fondly to cling around it, are not means of annoyance to you, but your country's own means of distinction and defence. All is peace; and God has granted you this sight of your country's happiness, ere you slumber in the grave forever. He has allowed you to behold and to partake the reward of your patriotic toils; and he has allowed us, your sons and countrymen, to meet you here, and in the name of the present generation, in the name of your country, in the name of liberty, to thank you!

But, alas! you are not all here! Time and the sword have thinned your ranks. Prescott, Putnam, Stark, Brooks, Read,

Pomeroy, Bridge! our eyes seek for you in vain amidst this broken band. You are gathered to your fathers, and live only to your country in her grateful remembrance, and your own bright example. But let us not too much grieve, that you
5 have met the common fate of men. You lived, at least, long enough to know that your work had been nobly and successfully accomplished. You lived to see your country's independence established, and to sheathe your swords from war. On the light of Liberty you saw arise the light of Peace, like

> ' another morn,
> Risen on mid-noon ; ' —

and the sky, on which you closed your eyes, was cloudless.
But — ah ! — Him ! the first great Martyr in this great cause ! Him ! the premature victim of his own self-devoting
15 heart ! Him ! the head of our civil councils, and the destined leader of our military bands ; whom nothing brought hither, but the unquenchable fire of his own spirit ; Him ! cut off by Providence, in the hour of overwhelming anxiety and thick gloom ; falling, ere he saw the star of his country rise ; pouring out his
20 generous blood, like water, before he knew whether it would fertilize a land of freedom or of bondage ! how shall I struggle with the emotions, that stifle the utterance of thy name ! — Our poor work may perish ; but thine shall endure ! This monument may moulder away ; the solid ground it rests upon may
25 sink down to a level with the sea ; but thy memory shall not fail ! Wheresoever among men a heart shall be found, that beats to the transports of patriotism and liberty, its aspirations shall be to claim kindred with thy spirit !

But the scene amidst which we stand does not permit us
30 to confine our thoughts or our sympathies to those fearless spirits, who hazarded or lost their lives on this consecrated spot. We have the happiness to rejoice here in the presence

of a most worthy representation of the survivors of the whole Revolutionary Army.

VETERANS ! you are the remnant of many a well fought field. You bring with you marks of honor from Trenton and Monmouth, from Yorktown, Camden, Bennington, and Saratoga. VETERANS OF HALF A CENTURY ! when in your youthful days, you put every thing at hazard in your country's cause, good as that cause was, and sanguine as youth is, still your fondest hopes did not stretch onward to an hour like this ! At a period to which you could not reasonably have expected to arrive ; at a moment of national prosperity, such as you could never have foreseen, you are now met, here, to enjoy the fellowship of old soldiers, and to receive the overflowings of an universal gratitude.

But your agitated countenances and your heaving breasts inform me that even this is not an unmixed joy. I perceive that a tumult of contending feelings rushes upon you. The images of the dead, as well as the persons of the living, throng to your embraces. The scene overwhelms you, and I turn from it. May the Father of all mercies smile upon your declining years, and bless them ! And when you shall here have exchanged your embraces ; when you shall once more have pressed the hands which have been so often extended to give succour in adversity, or grasped in the exultation of victory ; then look abroad into this lovely land, which your young valor defended, and mark the happiness with which it is filled ; yea, look abroad into the whole earth, and see what a name you have contributed to give to your country, and what a praise you have added to freedom, and then rejoice in the sympathy and gratitude, which beam upon your last days from the improved condition of mankind.

The occasion does not require of me any particular account of the battle of the 17th of June, nor any detailed narrative of

the events which immediately preceded it.   These are fami-
liarly known to all.   In the progress of the great and interesting controversy, Massachusetts and the town of Boston had
become early and marked objects of the displeasure of the
5 British Parliament.   This had been manifested, in the Act for
altering the Government of the Province, and in that for shutting up the Port of Boston.   Nothing sheds more honor on our
early history, and nothing better shows how little the feelings
and sentiments of the colonies were known or regarded in
10 England, than the impression which these measures every where
produced in America.   It had been anticipated, that while the
other colonies would be terrified by the severity of the punishment inflicted on Massachusetts, the other seaports would be
governed by a mere spirit of gain ; and that, as Boston was
15 now cut off from all commerce, the unexpected advantage,
which this blow on her was calculated to confer on other
towns, would be greedily enjoyed.   How miserably such rea-
soners deceived themselves !   How little they knew of the
depth, and the strength, and the intenseness of that feeling
20 of resistance to illegal acts of power, which possessed the
whole American people !   Every where the unworthy boon
was rejected with scorn.   The fortunate occasion was seized,
every where, to show to the whole world, that the colonies were
swayed by no local interest, no partial interest, no selfish inter-
25 est.   The temptation to profit by the punishment of Boston
was strongest to our neighbours of Salem.   Yet Salem was precisely the place, where this miserable proffer was spurned, in
a tone of the most lofty self-respect, and the most indignant
patriotism.   'We are deeply affected,' said its inhabitants, 'with
30 the sense of our public calamities ; but the miseries that are
now rapidly hastening on our brethren in the capital of the
Province, greatly excite our commiseration.   By shutting up the
Port of Boston, some imagine that the course of trade might
be turned hither and to our benefit ; but we must be dead to

every idea of justice, lost to all feelings of humanity, could we indulge a thought to seize on wealth, and raise our fortunes on the ruin of our suffering neighbours.'   These noble sentiments were not confined to our immediate vicinity.   In that day of general affection and brotherhood, the blow given to Boston 5 smote on every patriotic heart, from one end of the country to the other.   Virginia and the Carolinas, as well as Connecticut and New Hampshire, felt and proclaimed the cause to be their own.   The Continental Congress, then holding its first session in Philadelphia, expressed its sympathy for the suffer- 10 ing inhabitants of Boston, and addresses were received from all quarters, assuring them that the cause was a common one, and should be met by common efforts and common sacrifices. The Congress of Massachusetts responded to these assur- ances ; and in an address to the Congress at Philadelphia, 15 bearing the official signature, perhaps among the last, of the immortal Warren, notwithstanding the severity of its suf- fering and the magnitude of the dangers which threatened it, it was declared, that this colony 'is ready, at all times, to spend and to be spent in the cause of America.'   20

But the hour drew nigh, which was to put professions to the proof, and to determine whether the authors of these mutual pledges were ready to seal them in blood.   The tidings of Lexington and Concord had no sooner spread, than it was universally felt, that the time was at last come for action.   A 25 spirit pervaded all ranks, not transient, not boisterous, but deep, solemn, determined,

'totamque infusa per artus
Mens agitat molem, et magno se corpore miscet.'

War, on their own soil and at their own doors, was, indeed, a 30 strange work to the yeomanry of New England ; but their consciences were convinced of its necessity, their country called them to it, and they did not withhold themselves from

3

the perilous trial. The ordinary occupations of life were abandoned; the plough was staid in the unfinished furrow; wives gave up their husbands, and mothers gave up their sons, to the battles of a civil war. Death might come, in honor, on
5 the field; it might come, in disgrace, on the scaffold. For either and for both they were prepared. The sentiment of Quincy was full in their hearts. 'Blandishments,' said that distinguished son of genius and patriotism, 'will not fascinate us, nor will threats of a halter intimidate; for, under God, we
10 are determined, that wheresoever, whensoever, or howsoever we shall be called to make our exit, we will die free men.'

The 17th of June saw the four New England colonies standing here, side by side, to triumph or to fall together; and there was with them from that moment to the end of the
15 war, what I hope will remain with them forever, one cause, one country, one heart.

The battle of Bunker Hill was attended with the most important effects beyond its immediate result as a military engagement. It created at once a state of open, public war.
20 There could now be no longer a question of proceeding against individuals, as guilty of treason or rebellion. That fearful crisis was past. The appeal now lay to the sword, and the only question was, whether the spirit and the resources of the people would hold out, till the object should be accomplished.
25 Nor were its general consequences confined to our own country. The previous proceedings of the colonies, their appeals, resolutions, and addresses, had made their cause known to Europe. Without boasting, we may say, that in no age or country, has the public cause been maintained with more force of argument,
30 more power of illustration, or more of that persuasion which excited feeling and elevated principle can alone bestow, than the revolutionary state papers exhibit. These papers will forever deserve to be studied, not only for the spirit which they breathe, but for the ability with which they were written.

To this able vindication of their cause, the colonies had now added a practical and severe proof of their own true devotion to it, and evidence also of the power which they could bring to its support. All now saw, that if America fell, she would not fall without a struggle. Men felt sympathy and regard, as well as surprise, when they beheld these infant states, remote, unknown, unaided, encounter the power of England, and in the first considerable battle, leave more of their enemies dead on the field, in proportion to the number of combatants, than they had recently known in the wars of Europe.

Information of these events, circulating through Europe, at length reached the ears of one who now hears me. He has not forgotten the emotion, which the fame of Bunker Hill, and the name of Warren, excited in his youthful breast.

Sir, we are assembled to commemorate the establishment of great public principles of liberty, and to do honor to the distinguished dead. The occasion is too severe for eulogy to the living. But, sir, your interesting relation to this country, the peculiar circumstances which surround you and surround us, call on me to express the happiness which we derive from your presence and aid in this solemn commemoration.

Fortunate, fortunate man! with what measure of devotion will you not thank God, for the circumstances of your extraordinary life! You are connected with both hemispheres and with two generations. Heaven saw fit to ordain, that the electric spark of Liberty should be conducted, through you, from the new world to the old; and we, who are now here to perform this duty of patriotism, have all of us long ago received it in charge from our fathers to cherish your name and your virtues. You will account it an instance of your good fortune, sir, that you crossed the seas to visit us at a time which enables you to be present at this solemnity. You now behold the field, the renown of which reached you in the

heart of France, and caused a thrill in your ardent bosom. You see the lines of the little redoubt thrown up by the in- credible diligence of Prescott; defended, to the last extrem- ity, by his lion-hearted valor; and within which the corner
5 stone of our monument has now taken its position. You see where Warren fell, and where Parker, Gardner, McCleary, Moore, and other early patriots fell with him. Those who survived that day, and whose lives have been prolonged to the present hour, are now around you. Some of them you have
10 known in the trying scenes of the war. Behold! they now stretch forth their feeble arms to embrace you. Behold! they raise their trembling voices to invoke the blessing of God on you, and yours, forever.

Sir, you have assisted us in laying the foundation of this edi-
15 fice. You have heard us rehearse, with our feeble commenda- tion, the names of departed patriots. Sir, monuments and eulogy belong to the dead. We give them, this day, to War- ren and his associates. On other occasions they have been given to your more immediate companions in arms, to Wash-
20 ington, to Greene, to Gates, Sullivan, and Lincoln. Sir, we have become reluctant to grant these, our highest and last honors, further. We would gladly hold them yet back from the little remnant of that immortal band. *Serus in cœlum redeas.* Illustrious as are your merits, yet far, oh, very far dis-
25 tant be the day, when any inscription shall bear your name, or any tongue pronounce its eulogy!

The leading reflection, to which this occasion seems to in- vite us, respects the great changes which have happened in the fifty years, since the battle of Bunker Hill was fought. And
30 it peculiarly marks the character of the present age, that, in looking at these changes, and in estimating their effect on our condition, we are obliged to consider, not what has been done in our own country only, but in others also. In these interest-

ing times, while nations are making separate and individual advances in improvement, they make, too, a common progress; like vessels on a common tide, propelled by the gales at different rates, according to their several structure and management, but all moved forward by one mighty current beneath, 5 strong enough to bear onward whatever does not sink beneath it.

28 A chief distinction of the present day is a community of opinions and knowledge amongst men, in different nations, existing in a degree heretofore unknown. Knowledge has, in our 10 time, triumphed, and is triumphing, over distance, over difference of languages, over diversity of habits, over prejudice, and over bigotry. The civilized and Christian world is fast learning the great lesson, that difference of nation does not imply necessary hostility, and that all contact need not be war. The 15 whole world is becoming a common field for intellect to act in. Energy of mind, genius, power, wheresoever it exists, may speak out in any tongue, and the *world* will hear it. A great chord of sentiment and feeling runs through two continents, and vibrates over both. Every breeze wafts intelligence from 20 country to country; every wave rolls it; all give it forth, and all in turn receive it. There is a vast commerce of ideas; there are marts and exchanges for intellectual discoveries. and a wonderful fellowship of those individual intelligences which make up the mind and opinion of the age. Mind is the great 25 lever of all things; human thought is the process by which human ends are ultimately answered; and the diffusion of knowledge, so astonishing in the last half century, has rendered innumerable minds, variously gifted by nature, competent to be competitors, or fellow-workers, on the theatre of 30 intellectual operation.

29 From these causes, important improvements have taken place in the personal condition of individuals. Generally speaking, mankind are not only better fed, and better clothed,

but they are able also to enjoy more leisure; they possess
more refinement and more self-respect. A superior tone of
education, manners, and habits prevails. This remark, most
true in its application to our own country, is also partly true,
5 when applied elsewhere. It is proved by the vastly augmented consumption of those articles of manufacture and of
commerce, which contribute to the comforts and the decencies
of life; an augmentation which has far outrun the progress of
population.   And while the unexampled and almost incredible
10 use of machinery would seem to supply the place of labor,
labor still finds its occupation and its reward; so wisely has
Providence adjusted men's wants and desires to their condition and their capacity.

30 Any adequate survey, however, of the progress made in the
15 last half century, in the polite and the mechanic arts, in machinery and manufactures, in commerce and agriculture, in
letters and in science, would require volumes.   I must abstain
wholly from these subjects, and turn, for a moment, to the
contemplation of what has been done on the great question of
20 politics and government.   This is the master topic of the age;
and during the whole fifty years, it has intensely occupied the
thoughts of men.   The nature of civil government, its ends and
uses, have been canvassed and investigated; ancient opinions
attacked and defended; new ideas recommended and resisted,
25 by whatever power the mind of man could bring to the controversy.   From the closet and the public halls the debate has
been transferred to the field; and the world has been shaken
by wars of unexampled magnitude, and the greatest variety of
fortune.   A day of peace has at length succeeded; and now
30 that the strife has subsided, and the smoke cleared away, we
may begin to see what has actually been done, permanently
changing the state and condition of human society.   And
without dwelling on particular circumstances, it is most apparent, that, from the beforementioned causes of augmented

knowledge and improved individual attention, a real, substantial, and important change has taken place, and is taking place, greatly beneficial, on the whole, to human liberty and human happiness.

The great wheel of political revolution began to move in America. Here its rotation was guarded, regular, and safe. Transferred to the other continent, from unfortunate but natural causes, it received an irregular and violent impulse; it whirled along with a fearful celerity; till at length, like the chariot wheels in the races of antiquity, it took fire from the rapidity of its own motion, and blazed onward, spreading conflagration and terror around.

We learn from the result of this experiment, how fortunate was our own condition, and how admirably the character of our people was calculated for making the great example of popular governments. The possession of power did not turn the heads of the American people, for they had long been in the habit of exercising a great portion of self-control. Although the paramount authority of the parent state existed over them, yet a large field of legislation had always been open to our colonial assemblies. They were accustomed to representative bodies and the forms of free government; they understood the doctrine of the division of power among different branches, and the necessity of checks on each. The character of our countrymen, moreover, was sober, moral, and religious; and there was little in the change to shock their feelings of justice and humanity, or even to disturb an honest prejudice. We had no domestic throne to overturn, no privileged orders to cast down, no violent changes of property to encounter. In the American Revolution, no man sought or wished for more than to defend and enjoy his own. None hoped for plunder or for spoil. Rapacity was unknown to it; the axe was not among the instruments of its accomplishment; and we all know that it could not have lived a single day under any well founded imputation of possessing a tendency adverse to the Christian religion.

It need not surprise us, that, under circumstances less auspicious, political revolutions elsewhere, even when well intended, have terminated differently. It is, indeed, a great achievement, it is the master work of the world, to establish governments entirely popular, on lasting foundations; nor is it easy, indeed, to introduce the popular principle at all, into governments to which it has been altogether a stranger. It cannot be doubted, however, that Europe has come out of the contest, in which she has been so long engaged, with greatly superior knowledge, and, in many respects, a highly improved condition. Whatever benefit has been acquired, is likely to be retained, for it consists mainly in the acquisition of more enlightened ideas. And although kingdoms and provinces may be wrested from the hands that hold them, in the same manner they were obtained; although ordinary and vulgar power may, in human affairs, be lost as it has been won; yet it is the glorious prerogative of the empire of knowledge, that what it gains it never loses. On the contrary, it increases by the multiple of its own power; all its ends become means; all its attainments, helps to new conquests. Its whole abundant harvest is but so much seed wheat, and nothing has ascertained, and nothing can ascertain, the amount of ultimate product.

Under the influence of this rapidly increasing knowledge, the people have begun, in all forms of government, to think, and to reason, on affairs of state. Regarding government as an institution for the public good, they demand a knowledge of its operations, and a participation in its exercise. A call for the Representative system, wherever it is not enjoyed, and where there is already intelligence enough to estimate its value, is perseveringly made. Where men may speak out, they demand it; where the bayonet is at their throats, they pray for it.

When Louis XIV said, " I am the state," he expressed the essence of the doctrine of unlimited power. By the rules of that system, the people are disconnected from the state; they are its subjects; it is their lord. These ideas, founded in the love of power, and long supported by the excess and the abuse 5 of it, are yielding, in our age, to other opinions; and the civilized world seems at last to be proceeding to the conviction of that fundamental and manifest truth, that the powers of government are but a trust, and that they cannot be lawfully exercised but for the good of the community. As knowledge is 10 more and more extended, this conviction becomes more and more general. Knowledge, in truth, is the great sun in the firmament. Life and power are scattered with all its beams. The prayer of the Grecian combatant, when enveloped in unnatural clouds and darkness, is the appropriate political suppli- 15 cation for the people of every country not yet blessed with free institutions;

> ' Dispel this cloud, the light of heaven restore,
> Give me TO SEE —— and Ajax asks no more.'

We may hope, that the growing influence of enlightened 20 sentiments will promote the permanent peace of the world. Wars, to maintain family alliances, to uphold or to cast down dynasties, to regulate successions to thrones, which have occupied so much room in the history of modern times, if not less likely to happen at all, will be less likely to become general and 25 involve many nations, as the great principle shall be more and more established, that the interest of the world is peace, and its first great statute, that every nation possesses the power of establishing a government for itself. But public opinion has attained also an influence over governments, which do not 30 admit the popular principle into their organization. A necessary respect for the judgment of the world operates, in some measure, as a control over the most unlimited forms of authority.

It is owing, perhaps, to this truth, that the interesting struggle
of the Greeks has been suffered to go on so long, without a
direct interference, either to wrest that country from its present masters, and add it to other powers, or to execute the
5 system of pacification by force, and, with united strength, lay
the neck of christian and civilized Greece at the foot of the
barbarian Turk.   Let us thank God that we live in an age,
when something has influence besides the bayonet, and when
the sternest authority does not venture to encounter the scorch-
10 ing power of public reproach.   Any attempt of the kind I have
mentioned, should be met by one universal burst of indigna-
tion; the air of the civilized world ought to be made too warm
to be comfortably breathed by any who would hazard it.

It is, indeed, a touching reflection, that while, in the fulness
15 of our country's happiness, we rear this monument to her
honor, we look for instruction, in our undertaking, to a country
which is now in fearful contest, not for works of art or memo-
rials of glory, but for her own existence.   Let her be assured,
that she is not forgotten in the world; that her efforts are
20 applauded, and that constant prayers ascend for her success.
And let us cherish a confident hope for her final triumph.   If
the true spark of religious and civil liberty be kindled, it will
burn.   Human agency cannot extinguish it.   Like the earth's
central fire it may be smothered for a time; the ocean may
25 overwhelm it; mountains may press it down; but its inherent
and unconquerable force will heave both the ocean and the
land, and at some time or another, in some place or another,
the volcano will break out and flame up to heaven.

Among the great events of the half century, we must reckon,
30 certainly, the Revolution of South America; and we are not
likely to overrate the importance of that Revolution, either to
the people of the country itself or to the rest of the world.
The late Spanish colonies, now independent states, under circumstances less favorable, doubtless, than attended our own

Revolution, have yet successfully commenced their national existence. They have accomplished the great object of establishing their independence; they are known and acknowledged in the world; and although in regard to their systems of government, their sentiments on religious toleration, and their provisions for public instruction, they may have yet much to learn, it must be admitted that they have risen to the condition of settled and established states, more rapidly than could have been reasonably anticipated. They already furnish an exhilirating example of the difference between free governments and despotic misrule. Their commerce, at this moment, creates a new activity in all the great marts of the world. They show themselves able, by an exchange of commodities, to bear an useful part in the intercourse of nations. A new spirit of enterprise and industry begins to prevail; all the great interests of society receive a salutary impulse; and the progress of information not only testifies to an improved condition, but constitutes, itself, the highest and most essential improvement.

When the battle of Bunker Hill was fought, the existence of South America was scarcely felt in the civilized world. The thirteen little colonies of North America habitually called themselves the 'Continent.' Borne down by colonial subjugation, monopoly, and bigotry, these vast regions of the South were hardly visible above the horizon. But in our day there hath been, as it were, a new creation. The Southern Hemisphere emerges from the sea. Its lofty mountains begin to lift themselves into the light of heaven; its broad and fertile plains stretch out, in beauty, to the eye of civilized man, and at the mighty bidding of the voice of political liberty the waters of darkness retire.

And, now, let us indulge an honest exultation in the conviction of the benefit, which the example of our country has produced, and is likely to produce, on human freedom and human happiness. And let us endeavour to comprehend, in all its magnitude, and to feel, in all its importance, the part assigned to us in the great drama of human affairs. We are placed at the head of the system of representative and popular governments. Thus far our example shows, that such governments are compatible, not only with respectability and power, but with repose, with peace, with security of personal rights, with good laws, and a just administration.

We are not propagandists. Wherever other systems are preferred, either as being thought better in themselves, or as better suited to existing condition, we leave the preference to be enjoyed. Our history hitherto proves, however, that the popular form is practicable, and that with wisdom and knowledge men may govern themselves; and the duty incumbent on us is, to preserve the consistency of this cheering example, and take care that nothing may weaken its authority with the world. If, in our case, the Representative system ultimately fail, popular governments must be pronounced impossible. No combination of circumstances more favorable to the experiment can ever be expected to occur. The last hopes of mankind, therefore, rest with us; and if it should be proclaimed, that our example had become an argument against the experiment, the knell of popular liberty would be sounded throughout the earth.

These are excitements to duty; but they are not suggestions of doubt. Our history and our condition, all that is gone before us, and all that surrounds us, authorize the belief, that popular governments, though subject to occasional variations, perhaps not always for the better, in form, may yet, in their general character, be as durable and permanent as other systems. We know, indeed, that, in our country, any other is impossible. The *Principle* of Free Governments adheres to the American soil. It is bedded in it; immovable as its mountains.

And let the sacred obligations which have devolved on this generation, and on us, sink deep into our hearts. Those are daily dropping from among us, who established our liberty and our government. The great trust now descends to new hands. Let us apply ourselves to that which is presented to us, as our appropriate object. We can win no laurels in a war for Independence. Earlier and worthier hands have gathered them all. Nor are there places for us by the side of Solon, and Alfred, and other founders of states. Our fathers have filled them. But there remains to us a great duty of defence and preservation; and there is opened to us, also, a noble pursuit, to which the spirit of the times strongly invites us. Our proper business is improvement. Let our age be the age of improvement. In a day of peace, let us advance the arts of peace and the works of peace. Let us develop the resources of our land, call forth its powers, build up its institutions, promote all its great interests, and see whether we also, in our day and generation, may not perform something worthy to be remembered. Let us cultivate a true spirit of union and harmony. In pursuing the great objects, which our condition points out to us, let us act under a settled conviction, and an habitual feeling, that these twenty-four states are one country. Let our conceptions be enlarged to the circle of our duties. Let us extend our ideas over the whole of the vast field in which we are called to act. Let our object be, OUR COUNTRY, OUR WHOLE COUNTRY, AND NOTHING BUT OUR COUNTRY. And, by the blessing of God, may that country itself become a vast and splendid Monument, not of oppression and terror, but of Wisdom, of Peace and of Liberty, upon which the world may gaze, with admiration, forever!

NOTES

WASHINGTON'S FAREWELL ADDRESS

The Text: the text of the *Farewell Address* is that of its original appearance in the *American Daily Advertiser*, a file of which is to be found in the Lenox Library. Though I have copied the text from the newspaper, I have compared this version with the private reprint of the Washington manuscript, made by James Lenox in 1850; the reprint made by the Empire State Society, Sons of the American Revolution, September 19, 1896; an edition published by John Tiebout in New York in 1796; editions printed by Ormrod and Conrad, and by Sweitzer and Ormrod in Philadelphia the same year, 1796, and the original manuscript itself, to which I have had access through the obliging courtesy of the librarian in charge of the Lenox Library, Mr. Wilberforce Eames.

In the newspaper, the address occupies the whole of the second page, five columns, and a column and a half of the third page. The Washington manuscript consists of thirty-two pages, with holes punched at the sides; the pages are tied together. Since both sides of the pages are written upon, the whole manuscript presents the appearance of a book. Capitals are used lavishly, though sometimes it is hard to tell whether Washington intended a capital or not. A period and a dash follow most of the sentences; frequently a dash follows a semicolon, a comma, or a question mark. Instead of a period there is a semicolon or a colon in a number of places at the end of a sentence. The sign & is used almost always instead of "and." Commas are used freely, especially before restrictive adjective clauses, where present usage prefers no mark of punctuation.

That the newspaper and the early reprints of the address are, on the whole, nearer the present-day usage in punctuation and spelling than the recent reprints from the manuscript or the manuscript itself is certain. An examination of the paragraph beginning "How far in the discharge," etc., for example, shows both spelling and punctuation substantially like present usage, but in the manuscript there are capitals for "Records" and "You"; there is a comma before "and to the world"; and there is a dash after "world." Since, therefore, it would be decidedly confusing to follow the manuscript precisely, and since the newspaper edition is nearer present usage and had the personal correction of the author (see page xxiv), I have followed that text except in a few obvious misprints, such as "reigns," page 9, line 6, where the MS. has the proper form "reins."

2 4 **an address**: see Introduction, page xx.

2 15 **the proper occasion**: viz., Washington's inauguration. See page xii.

2 19 **Not unconscious**: an attempt to give the syntax of "unconscious" will quickly reveal the dangling construction. If the sentence showed correct grammatical relationship, the pronoun *I* would need to be the subject of the verb, and there would need to be a complete reconstruction of the sentence.

2 28 **does not forbid it**: in the manuscript copy of the address there followed another sentence, as the last in the paragraph: "May I also have that of knowing in my retreat, that the involuntary errors, I have probably committed, have been the sources of no serious or lasting mischief to our country, I may then expect to realize, without alloy, the sweet enjoyment of partaking, in the midst of my fellow citizens, the benign influence of good laws under a free government; the ever favorite object of my heart, and the happy reward, I trust, of our mutual cares, dangers, and labours." Washington obliterated this "to avoid the imputation of affected modesty," as he notes in the margin of his manuscript.

3 26 **Here, perhaps, I ought to stop**: note the short, pointed sentence set between long, cumbersome sentences.

3 28 **an occasion like the present**: *i. e.*, Washington's announcement of his desire to leave the public service and not be considered as a possible choice for the presidency for a third term. Strictly there was no "occasion" at this time of the same kind as the occasion referred to in the first sentence of the fifth paragraph.

3 30 **sentiments**: other words used by the author either in the preliminary drafts of the address or in the final form printed here, in referring to the main thoughts of the address, are *counsels*, *subjects*, *topics*, *hints*, and *heads*. The sentence beginning, "But a solicitude for your welfare," contains the idea developed in the whole body of the address. In some early editions, extra space is left at the close of the seventh paragraph, in order to make the body stand out more clearly.

4 4 **a former and not dissimilar occasion**: Washington's parting words to Congress when he resigned as commander-in-chief of the army might perhaps be considered to be the reference here, but more probably his address to the governors of the states at the time of his resignation from the army is what he had in mind. See pages xi and xxi.

4 8 The Unity of Government: the first of the reflections or sentiments deals, it will be seen, with the principle of union in the government. How many paragraphs are devoted to this subject? Does what Washington says hold true now?

4 24 Palladium: in order not to miss Washington's meaning, consult a dictionary for the sense of this word, which is still frequently used. The reader should also make sure that he understands the meaning of *rankness*, as used in line 11, page 10.

4 31 For this: note the transition phrase inserted at the beginning of the paragraph. By such devices the writer secures continuity. Compare the transitional opening of the next paragraph; it will be noticed, in fact, that the entire eleventh paragraph is transitional, that it may be called a link paragraph. Compare note on "while we hold still," page 28, line 29. The transitional phrase in the last line of page 12 was not in the original draft; its insertion is an illuminating indication of the writer's regard for continuity in the revision of his paper.

4 34 American: in the original manuscript two lines are drawn under AMERICAN, which is a way of indicating to the printer that the word should be set in small capitals. Elsewhere in the address, too, where small capitals now appear they were indicated by the double underscoring in the manuscript which the first printers followed (cf. note on *North*, page 5, line 13):

5 2 any appellation: the diction in this sentence is decidedly heavy, in the Johnsonian manner characteristic of many American writers of the period. In the last sentence of the twelfth paragraph, the diction is still heavier.

5 10 your interest: the second leading reflection has to do with the unity of sections of the country, rather than with the unity of the government itself, which is developed in the first main section.

5 13 North: here in the manuscript by underscoring the word the writer indicated that he wished *North* to be set in italics. The same is true regarding other words which appear in italics. The present tendency is to gain emphasis not by a different kind of type but by arrangement of the words in the sentence; it is thought now that sufficient emphasis can be gained in this way, without the resort to italics. In the third from the last sentence of paragraph 26 (p. 12, l. 17), Washington underscored the word *desert*, but the printer put *oaths* in italics instead.

6 5 While then every part: more recent usage would put commas before and after "then," which in this place has the force not of time but of reason. This transitional word, it is worth noting, is inserted in the manuscript by a caret. In reading the address through in its entirety, the writer doubtless saw that a transitional word here would improve the continuity of his thought. In another place, also, page 12, line 30, the word *then* is similarly inserted by a caret for transitional effect. Notice the punctuation of the word " likewise," page 11, line 17, and page 14, line 25.

6 28 Let experience solve it : Washington had something of Burke's aversion to " mere speculation." Like Burke, Washington had misgivings about what Burke calls " paper government," good in theory, perhaps, but never tested in practice. See the whole of the third sentence of paragraph 18 (p. 9, l. 17), containing the statement " experience is the surest standard."

7 19 treaty with Spain : this is called the treaty of San Ildefonso. It was negotiated by Thomas Pinckney in 1795. Full details of how it affected the interests of the citizens of the Mississippi region can readily be found by those students who are carrying on advanced work in American history parallel with their study of this address. The treaty established the southern boundary of the United States, and secured the free navigation of the Mississippi River.

7 24 two treaties : the treaty with Spain has been already explained. For a statement of how the treaty with England favored the interests of the inhabitants of our western country, see page xvii.

8 4 better calculated than your former : the President believed the government established under the Constitution to be better suited to make a close union than the government established under the Articles of Confederation. See page xi.

8 8 mature deliberation : see Introduction, page xii.

8 34 digested by common councils : note the balance ending this sentence.

10 1 I have already intimated : see page 7, line 4. The nineteenth paragraph, consisting of two sentences, one of which looks back to a completed section of the address, and the other of which looks forward to a new group of ideas, may be called a link paragraph (cf. page 56).

10 13 domination of one faction over another : in Grecian, Roman, and English history there are illustrations of the truth of the statement by Washington that " enormities " have been perpetrated in " different ages and countries " through the alternate domination of one party or faction over another. So early as 427 B. C. there were bloody party contests in Corcyra (Greece), ending in the success of the democrats. In 88 B. C. began the war in Rome between the senatorial party of the optimates headed by Sulla and the popular party under Marius. The six-year struggle between these two parties was marked by a long series of murders; at one time three thousand prisoners were slaughtered at the command of Sulla. Conflict of parties resulted in lawless violence and public commotions in England in the time of Cromwell. Addison in an essay in *The Spectator* speaks of the feuds between the Roundheads and the Cavaliers, and says that a furious party spirit, when it rages in its full violence, exerts itself in civil war and bloodshed. He adds that Italy was long torn to pieces by the struggles of the two parties, Guelphs and Ghibellines.

11 4 There is an opinion: notice the method of Washington's argument. He refutes certain objections which he feels sure will be brought against the truth of his principal proposition.

11 14 A fire not to be quenched: how would you punctuate this last sentence of the paragraph?

11 20 avoiding . . . to encroach: the practice of the best writers of the present time is to use a verbal form in -ing after "avoid."

11 27 reciprocal checks: for years there have been efforts on the part of the Senate to resist encroachment upon their prerogatives by the President, and vice versa. In a speech delivered in the Senate in 1838 regarding the sudden political conversion of Calhoun, Webster referred in the following way to the conflict then existing between the executive and the legislative branches of the national government: "Here we all had been contending against the progress of Executive power, and more particularly and most strenuously, against the projects and experiments of the Administration upon the currency." According to current newspapers the President and the Senate are still serving as reciprocal checks in the exercise of political power. Moreover, within the national legislature it is not uncommon for the House to resent the attempted encroachments by the Senate upon its Constitutional function of originating revenue measures.

12 1 an amendment: experience has proved that the difficulty of making amendments to the Constitution is greater than the first President anticipated. How many amendments to the Constitution have been made, and under what circumstances?

12 30 institutions for the general diffusion of knowledge: see Introduction, page xiv.

13 2 sparingly: since this "address" was intended to be read, not spoken, it is particularly interesting to note a few of the corrections made by its author in revision. Here the word first written was "little." Then that was interlined, and the more specific and lively word "sparingly" substituted. In the next sentence "coincide" was written first, then stricken out in favor of "co-operate" which more accurately gives the shade of meaning desired. On page 14, line 8, the word "a" before "habitual" was replaced by "an." There is still diversity of usage in such cases as this. On page 17, line 3, the word "occasional," first written, gave way to "temporary" in the final form. The shade of meaning here also is much improved by the change.

13 16 inconvenient and unpleasant: see Introduction, page xv.

13 23 Observe good faith: President McKinley used the first two sentences of this paragraph as his text for an eloquent commendation of Washington's foreign policy. Extracts from the McKinley address show, better than any other commentary that I can think of, the continuing value and influence of Washington's sentiments: "To-day, nearly a century from Washington's death, we turn reverentially to study the leading principles of that comprehensive chart for the guidance of the people. It was his unflinching, immovable devotion to these perceptions of duty which more than anything else made him what he was, and contributed so directly to make us what we are. Following the precepts of Washington, we cannot err. The wise lessons in government which he left us it will be profitable to heed. He seems to have grasped all possible conditions and pointed the way safely to meet them. He has established danger signals all along the pathway of the nation's march. . . . His wisdom and foresight have been confirmed and vindicated after more than a century of experience."

14 3 nothing is more essential: study the clear method of thought-development followed by Washington in the elaboration of this sentence. Notice that on page 15, in the sentence beginning "Excessive partiality for one foreign nation," the same idea announced on page 14 is re-stated, after it has been developed fully. Thus the idea is firmly clinched.

14 7 The Nation: the phrasing in this sentence is by no means happy. Could you suggest a rearrangement of the words, or a reconstruction of the sentence, to make the idea a little clearer?

15 19 insidious wiles of foreign influence: see page xvi.

16 29 existing engagements: such, for instance, as the treaties with England and Spain referred to above.

17 7 neither seeking nor granting: what other participles in this long and complicated sentence are in the same grammatical construction as these two? Note that "rules" is the object of "establishing."

17 25 a just pride: Washington's tactful appeal to the self-respect of the people shows plainly his skill in winning supporters to any policy which he had at heart. See also the opening sentence of paragraph 48, where there is another kind of appeal, often effective in argument.

18 10 them: to what noun does this pronoun refer?

18 11 the still subsisting war in Europe: in 1796 Napoleon Bonaparte carried on a brilliant campaign in Italy against the Austrians. This same year, too, Spain declared war on England. The proclamation to which Washington refers declared the American policy in the crisis of 1793, the war between England and France, to be one of strict neutrality. See paragraphs 45–48, page 18, line 17, through page 19, line 5. From the fact that the President placed his discussion of the proper attitude of America to Europe last among the number of his counsels, and then selected this topic as an illustration of such of his own acts as carried out his sentiments it can easily be seen how deeply he felt on the subject of the young nation's foreign relations. Lodge, in his *George Washington*, has an excellent chapter of about ninety pages headed " Foreign Relations."

18 13 Sanctioned: what is the syntax of this participle ?

19 20 for several generations: see Introduction, page v.

19 28 17th September: see Introduction, page xxiv.

WEBSTER'S FIRST BUNKER HILL ORATION

The Text: after examination of a number of different editions of the address, the editor has chosen to follow exactly the text of 1825 (Lenox Library, New York). The other texts particularly examined were that of 1851, printed the year before Webster's death, and the second, third, and fifth editions, found in the Lenox Library, the Astor Library, and the library of the British Museum. The editions of 1825 are practically identical; for example, at the bottom of page 25 in each a period is raised somewhat above the line, and a hyphen has dropped out at the end of the line. On the whole, it has seemed best to print the earliest text. There are peculiarities of punctuation, of course, in the earliest edition, but these will not prove confusing. In fact, it will be a good exercise to notice the punctuation of restrictive adjective clauses, and the punctuation of substantive clauses, in which early usage differs from that of the present ; and the lavish use of semicolons and exclamation points. The modern tendency is to eliminate punctuation wherever it is possible to do so without causing confusion, and to use exclamation points sparingly. The reader should be on the outlook for what seem peculiarities in punctuation in the early text printed here. In spelling, too, there are a few oddities, judged by the standard of the latest dictionaries ; for instance, " any thing " written as two words. In spite of these differences, however, there is nothing to give anyone real trouble. The changes in diction in the 1851 edition, interesting as a revelation of how the author looked at his address years after it was first delivered and published, are not of any real significance, for the most part. They have nothing like the value of the changes made by Coleridge in his *Ancient Mariner* in the period between his text of 1798 and that of 1829. It therefore seems wise to follow the earliest available text of Webster's speech. In the original edition there is extra space between the main divisions of the address; this spacing has been retained in the present edition.

25 1 the shore of Plymouth: the date of the landing of the Pilgrims on Plymouth Rock scarcely needs to be given. For a reference to an oration of Webster's on the theme of the early settlement of New England, see page xxxi.

25 2 another early and ancient colony: the reference here is probably to the colony of Virginia, in which was situated the early settled town of Jamestown. It was a favorite idea of Webster's to couple the settlements at Jamestown and at Plymouth; he makes the reference twice in his oration of 1851 at the laying of the corner stone of the addition to the Capitol, at Washington, and in the same oration he addresses the "men of James River and the Bay, places consecrated by the early settlement of their commonwealth." However, Hale thinks the reference in the Bunker Hill speech is to the Maryland Colony, founded at St. Mary's in 1633.

25 23 solemnities suited to the occasion: see Introduction, page xl.

25 27 rising high: the monument is a granite shaft two hundred and twenty-one feet high, and thirty feet square at the base. By means of a spiral stairway inside the monument, one can climb to the circular chamber at the top; there is no elevator, but the climb is not particularly arduous. The cost of the structure was about $120,000, the cost of fencing and grading about $19,000, and the other expenses were about $17,000. The expense account for the ceremony of laying the corner stone was $4,720.85. In 1843, on the completion of the edifice, Webster referred to the high natural eminence on which the Bunker Hill Monument is placed, and said that the monument was visible at their homes to three hundred thousand of the people of Massachusetts. Now, however, in spite of the height and "unadorned grandeur" of the shaft, it is not Bunker Hill Monument that particularly attracts the gaze of the person approaching Boston, but rather the gilded dome of the State House. In fact, it must be acknowledged that Bunker Hill Monument seems now a little disappointing to one who sees it for the first time.

26 6 entablatures: consult dictionary for the meaning of this architectural term.

27 15 **till it meet:** note the force of the subjunctive, and compare "If . . . the Representative system ultimately *fail*," page 44, lines 18–19.

27 25 **twenty-four . . . states:** besides the thirteen original colonies — New Hampshire, Massachusetts, Rhode Island, Connecticut, New York, New Jersey, Pennsylvania, Delaware, Maryland, Virginia, North Carolina, South Carolina, and Georgia — each of which became a state — there had been formed either from part of the territory of some of the original states or from territory developed and populated later, eleven other states at the time Webster spoke, viz., Vermont (from New York), 1791; Kentucky (from Virginia), 1792; Tennessee (from North Carolina), 1796; Ohio (created), 1802; Louisiana (bought from France in 1803), 1812; Indiana (created), 1816; Mississippi (from Georgia), 1817; Illinois (created), 1818; Alabama (from Georgia), 1819; Maine (from Massachusetts), 1820; and Missouri (from Louisiana), 1821.

27 32 **the arm of successful industry:** Webster's use of figurative language to embellish his thought is decidedly interesting as exhibited in this address. In the first paragraph he spoke of the spacious temple of the firmament when he might have said simply the open air. What did he gain by the embroidered expression? What is the name of the figure? Again in the seventh paragraph he said that he hoped labor would be proud in the midst of its toil, when he meant the laboring man. What was the use of this decoration in language? Now, in saying the arm of industry, when he means the arm of the worker, the frontiersman, he makes still another departure from plain, literal statement. It is perhaps worth while to label all these departures from strict literalness, and so gain specific knowledge of the names of Webster's figures of speech; it is certainly desirable to consider the gain to his oration secured by these and other adornments which the reader will be pleased to notice. See the elaborate simile on page 37, and the striking and brilliant metaphors on pages 35 and 37. The metaphor on page 41 is also unusually original in its boldness. The simile on page 42 helps to make Webster's idea seem more forcible as well as clearer than a bare literal statement would have made it.

28 1 **become:** the syntax of this word is not apparent at a glance. It would be a little more effective English, because clearer, to write *have become* here, instead of "become" alone, which forces the reader to look back and find the "have."

28 3 **no sea unexplored:** compare Burke's *Conciliation*, "No sea but what is vexed by their fisheries."

28 11 **dashed against one another thrones:** the French Revolution and the Napoleonic wars disturbed monarchs of all Europe so that they feared for the security of their thrones. There was, as it were, a great earthquake which shook the thrones and sent them crashing down together. That is what Webster means by saying that the revolution in Europe dashed thrones against each other. The word thrones stands for the kings who occupied the thrones. What is the name of this figure of speech? Among the monarchs who trembled lest they might lose their kingdoms were Charles IV of Spain and Ferdinand IV of Naples. Charles IV abdicated in March, 1808, in favor of his son, and then both were compelled by Napoleon to renounce the throne a few months later. About the same time Ferdinand of Naples was also dethroned by Napoleon, the throne being then given to Napoleon's brother.

28 15 from beyond the track of the sun: *i. e.*, from Central and South America. Vertical rays of the sun describe on the earth, as it turns on its axis, a great circle, the Tropic of Cancer, which might be called the track of the sun. South of this would be the American republics referred to by Webster as struggling into existence with unaccustomed sounds of liberty. As early as 1823 the Central American Confederation was established, including Honduras, Guatemala, etc.; and not long after 1825 these free states became independent republics. In South America (cf. p. 42, l. 33), Chile proclaimed its independence of Spain in 1818, Peru in 1821. Peru finally defeated the Spanish viceroy only a few months before Webster spoke. As Webster says, there were sounds of liberty to the south; as the historians explain, there were in the first quarter of the century successful Central and South American rebellions of numerous Spanish and Portuguese colonies.

28 18 annihilated forever: for a reference to the American policy which helped to make permanent the elimination of European power on the American continent, see Introduction, page xxxi. President Monroe's Message to Congress in 1823 enunciated the doctrine that bears his name.

28 29 while we hold still: Webster's transitions in this oration are exceedingly deft. It is a keen pleasure to notice how in a number of places he skillfully prepares the way for the introduction of a new line of thought, what might be termed a new section of his speech. Here, by the long clause of time beginning with "while we hold still," he prepares for his touching and fervid direct address to the survivors of the battle. Again, on page 30, line 5, he leads the way to his apostrophe to Warren by three transition sentences, beautifully constructed, beginning, "You lived, at least, long enough to know." A similarly effective transition, too, may be seen in paragraph 15 (p. 30, l. 29), a short paragraph wholly transitional. Paragraph 23 (p. 35, l. 11), also serves as a link between two main divisions of the oration.

28 30 **from every quarter of New England:** see Introduction, page xxxix. In his address delivered in 1843, on the occasion of the completion of the monument, Webster gives the names of thirteen venerable men then present who "bore arms for their country" either at Concord and Lexington or on Bunker Hill.

29 7 **the same ocean rolls:** this reference always puzzles students who understand the geographical situation, as explained on page xlviii of the Introduction. The fact is that Webster in this reference to the ocean is speaking in a large oratorical sense, unhampered by strict geography. The ocean could plainly be seen from Breed's Hill, but strictly does not roll by it.

29 10 **strewed:** is *strowed*, which is the form of the word printed in a later text, the form used at present?

29 27 **forever:** this word is omitted in the later text.

30 10 **another morn:** from Book V of Milton's *Paradise Lost*, lines 310 and 311.

30 13 **Him! the first great Martyr:** a glance through the celebrated apostrophe to General Warren shows clearly the method of the orator in this part of the speech. Though Webster planned the main lines beforehand, it is clear that he did not painstakingly work out all the details, but allowed himself a margin for truly extemporaneous thoughts. Speaking, in the third person, about Warren, who has been long dead, he suddenly shifts to a conception of this martyred patriot as if he were actually present, and addresses him directly, saying, "how shall I struggle with the emotions that stifle the utterance of *thy* name! Our poor work may perish; but *thine* shall endure!" Edward Everett, in commenting on this change of persons, from the third to the second, remarks that Webster could not be content merely to "pour forth fervors a week old." Bearing in the main the marks of premeditated oratory, the speech nevertheless has impromptu, emotional elements.

Regarding Warren himself little needs to be added to what has already been said in the Introduction, page l. A graduate of Harvard College (1759), he became a much beloved physician who heartily espoused the patriot cause. At the time of his death he was Grand Master of the Grand Lodge of Free-Masons of Massachusetts. It was for this reason that King Solomon's Lodge erected in his honor and to commemorate his associates the first monument on Bunker Hill. All who visit the present monument notice in the room at its base the model of that first monument erected to Warren.

30 31 **this consecrated spot:** it may seem a little far-fetched, but this place is as good as any in the speech for directing attention to Lincoln's Gettysburg address, the only American speech which can be compared with the Bunker Hill oration in effectiveness as commemorative oratory Lincoln says, "We cannot consecrate, we cannot hallow this ground." His whole oration, being short, may well be read at this point: —

"Four score and seven years ago, our fathers brought forth upon this continent a new nation, conceived in liberty, and dedicated to the proposition that all men are created equal. Now we are engaged in a great civil war, testing whether that nation — or any nation so conceived and so dedicated — can long endure. We are met on a great battle-field of that war. We have come to dedicate a portion of that field as a final resting-place of those who here gave their lives that that nation might live. It is altogether fitting and proper that we should do this. But, in a larger sense, we cannot dedicate, we cannot consecrate, we cannot hallow this ground. The brave men, living and dead, who struggled here, have consecrated it far above our power to add or detract. The world will little note, nor long remember, what we say here; but it can never forget what they did here.

"It is for us, the living, rather to be dedicated here to the unfinished work which they who fought here have thus far so nobly advanced. It is rather for us to be here dedicated to the great task remaining before us; that from these honored dead we take increased devotion to that cause for which they gave the last full measure of devotion; that we here highly resolve that these dead shall not have died in vain; that this nation shall, under God, have a new birth of freedom; and that government of the people, by the people, for the people, shall not perish from the earth."

31 3 **Veterans:** in his direct address to the Revolutionary soldiers who were present, the speaker uses the words "Venerable Men" for the survivors of Bunker Hill, and the term "Veterans" for those who fought in other battles of the war, but not at Bunker Hill. For the number of old soldiers present see Introduction, page xxxix.

31 19 **The scene overwhelms you:** see Introduction, page xliii.

32 2 **interesting:** does Webster show poverty in his vocabulary because he uses this word "interesting" in other places in the address, as on page 36, line 33 and on page 42, line 1.

32 5 **This had been manifested:** Volume IV of the six-volume edition of Bancroft's *History of the United States of America* or any good edition of Burke's "Conciliation" speech, for example, Lamont's, may be consulted for abundant details regarding the severe measures taken by Parliament to curb the Massachusetts spirit. Webster mentions only two measures, but there were several other enactments of similar intent. What Webster calls the "act for altering the government of the Province" was passed by Parliament May 11, 1774, and assented to by King George

III on the morning of the twentieth. Its exact title was " An Act for the better regulating the government of the province of Massachusetts Bay in New England." The act made obnoxious changes in the government, such as, (1) Providing for the appointment of the upper house of the legislature, called the council, by the crown, whereas it had formerly been elected by the lower house, (2) Giving to the royal governor the appointment of judges, magistrates, sheriffs, (3) Putting the selection of jurymen into the hands of the sheriffs, instead of the people by regular election, as before, (4) Forbidding the holding of town meetings not sanctioned by the governor. The Boston Port Bill, which was passed in March of the same year, unanimously, in both the house of lords and the house of commons, reached Boston May 10, and was put into effect the first of the following month. It provided for the closing of the port of Boston, the transferring of the board of customs to Marblehead, and the seat of government to Salem. In three weeks from the time the act was received the whole continent made the cause of Boston its own. Another of the repressive measures was the act providing for the trial in England, or elsewhere outside of Massachusetts, of any person accused of murder or other capital offense, if the crime appeared to have been committed in helping a magistrate suppress disorder, in other words, if it had been committed in aiding the government.

33 9 **The Continental Congress:** see Introduction, page ix.

33 25 **was . . . come:** the present feeling for language is to say *had* instead of *was* in such expressions.

33 28 **totamque infusa . . . miscet:** from Vergil's *Æneid*, VI, 726, which may be translated, " an intelligence infused through the members of the universe actuates the whole frame and mingles with the great body of the universe." Conington's free poetical translation is —

> A bright intelligence, which darts
> Its influence through the several parts
> And animates the whole.

34 6 **The sentiment of Quincy:** Josiah Quincy was one of the most eloquent agitators in behalf of the popular cause from about 1767 till his death in 1775.

34 32 **the revolutionary state papers:** Webster explains this expression himself, a few lines above, in mentioning the appeals, resolutions, and addresses of the colonies, yet readers nearly always fail to see that the term " revolutionary state papers " means the same as " appeals, resolutions, and addresses."

35 10 **wars of Europe:** in the quarter century before the American Revolution there were, on the Continent, numerous battles engaged in by Frederic of Prussia against the French and Austrians, such as Rossbach in 1757; and against the Austrians and Russians, such as the Frankfort-on-the-Oder engagement of 1761. There were wars, too, against the Turks, waged by Russia (Ploetz's *Epitome of Ancient, Mediæval, and Modern History*, translated by Tillinghast). The number of casualties in these battles, Webster explains, was not so great, compared with the number of men engaged, as the casualties in the Bunker Hill battle. For the proportion in that contest, see page li.

35 14 **his youthful breast:** Lafayette was born in 1757.

35 17 **severe:** consult a large dictionary to find a meaning for "severe" that will precisely fit this context.

36 23 **Serus in cœlum redeas:** part of a line from the Latin poet, Horace, Book I, Ode 2, line 45, which means, when translated freely: may it be long before you return to the skies.

36 30 **character of the present age:** compare the first sentence of paragraph 8. It is worth while to study the duplication of thought in the third and seventh main divisions of the speech. A comparison of the vivid explanation, in this address, of the changes since the battle with the dry, statistical information on a similar subject in a later oration, in 1851, at the laying of the corner stone of the addition to the Capitol, reveals the difference between emotional, oratorical utterance and business-like facts. In the 1851 speech Webster says, "Since that time [the laying of the corner stone of the Capitol by President Washington, 18 September, 1793] astonishing changes have been wrought in the condition and prospects of the American people; and a degree of progress witnessed with which the world can furnish no parallel." The table which he then gives to explain this idea shows the number of states in 1793 compared with the number in 1851, tells the population of seven large cities at the two dates, the comparative imports, exports, Treasury receipts, etc., making over a page of solid statistics. Such a difference in methods of public speaking helps to explain why the Bunker Hill address has won its place as a great oratorical effort while the 1851 address is not often read now.

36 30 **in looking at these changes:** notice that the participle grammatically depends on a subject which follows. Many blunders in school compositions result from lack of care in the management of the relation of participles. Webster is here a good model

37 10 **Knowledge has . . . triumphed:** the first quarter of the nineteenth century was remarkable for the development of inventions to annihilate distance: steamboats, railroads, the electric telegraph. The first railroad on the Western Continent, says Hale, was constructed to help in hurrying the building of the Bunker Hill Monument.

38 15 the polite and the mechanic arts : Webster's care in the details of expression amounts sometimes almost to pedantry. However, it is pleasing to notice such marks of care as the repetition of *the* before *mechanic* because that adjective does not have the same meaning as *polite*. Many writers are careless about this rule of rhetoric. All through this long paragraph there are interesting features of rhetorical skill. Observe the groups of twos, and the series of threes, *e. g.*, " in commerce and agriculture, in letters and in science "; " real, substantial, and important." Doubtless the reader has been noticing here and there the groupings of ideas in series of phrases, as for example back in the fifth paragraph, the last sentence. Sometimes this handling of ideas in phrases or clauses or sentences of similar structure produces what may be called repeated structure, as in paragraph 7 (p. 26, l. 22), " We consecrate . . . We rear . . . We come . . . We wish . . . We wish . . . We wish . . . We wish . . . We wish . . . We wish . . . We wish . . . . "

39 5 political revolution : notice the thought connection between the thirtieth and thirty-first paragraphs.

39 28 no domestic throne to overturn : the negative items in the rest of this paragraph exhibit the use of a valuable method of paragraph development, telling what is not true of the subject under discussion and so making plainer the significance of what is said to be true. The method of negation is often one of the best devices for explanation.

39 33 the axe = the guillotine. In France there was frightful bloodshed when the people endeavored to overturn the monarchy and cast down the privileged orders. More than twenty-eight hundred persons perished by the guillotine in the Place de la Concorde, Paris, between 21 January, 1793, and 3 May, 1795. Of course, there was nothing like this in America as a result of the war for freedom from England. Yet is it not true that the treatment of many of the loyalists or Tories was more severe than could be gathered from what Webster says?

40 6 the master work of the world : compare page 38, line 20.

41 1 Louis XIV : King of France, during one of the longest and most absolute reigns in history, 1643–1715. His famous saying, " *L'Etat, c'est moi,*" is translated by Webster, " I am the state." The King simply meant by this that he considered himself the absolute ruler of the nation, with unlimited power.

41 14 the Grecian combatant : *i. e.*, Ajax. In the 1851 edition " combatant " is changed to " champion." The quotation beginning " Dispel this cloud," appears with double instead of single quotes in the 1851 text. The quotation is translated from Book XVII of Homer's *Iliad*.

41 21 permanent peace of the world : what recent attempts have been made to establish peace permanently in the civilized world?

42 1 **the interesting struggle of the Greeks** : compare the first sentence of paragraph 37 (p. 42, l. 14). The Grecian war for independence from Turkey began in 1821. See Introduction, page xxxii, and consult Ploetz's *Epitome* or an encyclopædia for further details of the struggle.

42 26 **heave** = cause to stir, swell, or bulge upward (*Century Dictionary*, definition 5, under *heave*, transitive).

42 29 **half century** : this is a hyphenated word in the 1851 edition. Usage at present inclines to use no hyphen here. This paragraph is worth studying closely to see how the opening topic sentence is developed.

43 15 **A new spirit of enterprise** : this sentence begins a new paragraph in the 1851 text. Does the thirty-eighth paragraph lack unity? Ought it to be divided into two paragraphs, each having a central thought?

43 22 **thirteen little colonies** : compare page 55.

43 26 **hath been** : the old verb form lends an air of dignity, a touch of Biblical loftiness, to the orator's language. Observe, too, the rhythmical flow of the last clause of the paragraph, part of which might almost be scanned it runs so regularly in iambic and anapestic feet.

44 10 **propagandists** : persons devoting themselves to the spread of any system of principles (*Century Dictionary*).

44 19 **must be pronounced impossible** : by what method does Webster prove the truth of this assertion? Could this be called *a fortiori* reasoning?

44 26 **excitements** : would *incitements* be better?

44 30 **in form** : the phrasing in this long sentence is not of the best. Would the meaning be plainer if the comma after " form " were omitted? Would the idea seem clearer if " in form " preceded "perhaps "?

44 34 **bedded** : it is a diverting exercise in diction to try to think of a better word than "bedded" for this particular place in the sentence.

45 8 **Nor** : notice how transition is secured by the connectives in this paragraph. Is the paragraph unified?

45 8 **Solon, and Alfred** : information regarding the governments which were founded by Solon and Alfred can be easily gained by reference to Lippincott's *Pronouncing Dictionary of Biography and Mythology*, an almost indispensable reference book for school libraries.

45 22 **twenty-four states** : compare page 27 , line 25, and see note.

45 27 **a vast and splendid Monument** : compare page 25, and consider how skillfully Webster rounds out his oration by going back to an idea started at the beginning and clinching it at the end after all his exposition has made it entirely clear.

ANNOUNCEMENTS

STANDARD ENGLISH CLASSICS

	List price	Mailing price
Macaulay's Essay on Addison. (Smith)	$0.25	$0.30
Macaulay's Essays on Addison and Milton (in one volume). (Smith)	.30	.35
Macaulay's Lays of Ancient Rome. (Daniell)	.35	.40
Macaulay's Life of Samuel Johnson, with a Selection from his Essay on Johnson. (Hanson)	.25	.30
Milton's L'Allegro, Il Penseroso, Comus, and Lycidas. (Huntington)	.25	.30
Milton's Paradise Lost, Books I and II, and Lycidas. (Sprague)	.30	.35
Pope's Rape of the Lock and Other Poems. (Parrott)	.30	.35
Pope's Translation of the Iliad, Books I, VI, XXII, and XXIV. (Tappan)	.25	.30
Ruskin's Essays and Letters. (Hufford)	.60	.70
Ruskin's Sesame and Lilies. (Hufford)	.25	.30
Scott's Ivanhoe. (Lewis)	.50	.65
Scott's Lady of the Lake. (Ginn)	.35	.40
Scott's Quentin Durward. (Bruère)	.50	.60
Shakespeare's As You Like It. (Hudson)	.30	.35
Shakespeare's Henry V. (Hudson)	.30	.35
Shakespeare's Julius Cæsar. (Hudson)	.30	.35
Shakespeare's Macbeth. (Hudson)	.30	.35
Shakespeare's Merchant of Venice. (Hudson)	.30	.35
Shakespeare's Twelfth Night. (Hudson)	.30	.35
Spenser's Faerie Queene: Selections. (Litchfield)	.40	.45
Tennyson's Gareth and Lynette, Lancelot and Elaine, and the Passing of Arthur. (Boughton)	.25	.30
Tennyson's The Princess. (Cook)	.30	.35
Thackeray's History of Henry Esmond, Esq. (Moore)	.60	.70
Washington's Farewell Address and Webster's First Bunker Hill Oration. (Gaston)	.25	.30

GINN & COMPANY PUBLISHERS

STANDARD ENGLISH CLASSICS

IN THE NEW SERIES BINDING

THE STANDARD IN SCHOLARLY EDITING, HELPFUL INTER-PRETATION, ATTRACTIVENESS, CONVENIENCE, REASONABLENESS OF PRICE

IN EVERY WAY ADAPTED TO MEET THE

COLLEGE ENTRANCE REQUIREMENTS IN ENGLISH

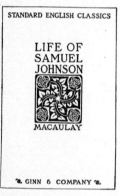

STANDARD ENGLISH CLASSICS

LIFE OF SAMUEL JOHNSON

MACAULAY

GINN & COMPANY

THE "Standard English Classics Series" has gained a very high standing throughout the country, largely because it fulfills admirably the three chief requirements of the discriminating teacher: *its volumes embody the highest editorial scholarship in introduction, notes, and other aids; they are attractively and substantially bound; and are offered at remarkably low prices.*

Recently the series has been made still more noteworthy by important changes made with the view of perfectly adapting the books for practical school use. Every excellent feature which has hitherto characterized the series has been carefully retained. In addition, the books now offer the double advantage of an unusually attractive and convenient semi-flexible cloth cover very clearly stamped in gold ink, and a considerable reduction in price.

GINN & COMPANY PUBLISHERS

STANDARD ENGLISH CLASSICS

	List price	Mailing price
Addison and Steele's Sir Roger de Coverley Papers. From "The Spectator." (Litchfield)	$0.30	$0.35
Blackmore's Lorna Doone. (Trent and Brewster)	.65	.8c
Browning, Elizabeth Barrett: Selections. (Lee)	.30	.35
Browning: Selections. (Lovett)	.30	.35
Bunyan's Pilgrim's Progress. (Montgomery)	.25	.30
Burke's Letter to a Noble Lord. (Smyth)	.30	.35
Burke's Speech on American Taxation. (Moffatt)	.25	.30
Burke's Speech on Conciliation with America. (Lamont)	.30	.35
Burns's Representative Poems, with Carlyle's Essay on Burns. (Hanson)	.30	.35
Carlyle's Essay on Burns. (Hanson)	.25	.30
Coleridge's Ancient Mariner. (Gibbs)	.20	.25
Cooper's Last of the Mohicans. (Dunbar)	.50	.60
De Quincey's English Mail-Coach and Joan of Arc. (Turk)	.25	.30
De Quincey's Revolt of the Tartars. (Simonds)	.25	.30
Dickens's Tale of Two Cities. (Linn)	.50	.60
Dryden's Palamon and Arcite. (Eliot)	.25	.30
Franklin's Autobiography. (Montgomery and Trent)	.40	.45
Gaskell's Cranford. (Simonds)	.30	.35
George Eliot's Silas Marner. (Witham)	.30	.35
Goldsmith's Deserted Village. (Pound)	.20	.25
Goldsmith's Vicar of Wakefield. (Montgomery)	.30	.35
Irving's Life of Goldsmith. (Gaston)	.40	.50
Irving's Sketch Book (Complete). (Litchfield)	.50	.60
Lamb, Essays of. (Wauchope)	.50	.60
Lamb's Essays of Elia. (Wauchope)	.40	.45
Macaulay's England in 1685. (Bates)	.30	.35
Macaulay's Essay on Milton. (Smith)	.20	.25

GINN & COMPANY PUBLISHERS

BOOKS ON
ENGLISH LITERATURE

	List price	Mailing price
Alexander's Introduction to the Poetry of Robert Browning	$1.00	$1.10
Athenæum Press Series: 26 volumes now ready.		
Baldwin's Inflections and Syntax of Malory's Morte d'Arthur	1.40	1.50
Bellamy's Twelve English Poets	.75	.85
Browne's Shakspere's Versification	.25	
Corson's Primer of English Verse	1.00	1.10
Emery's Notes on English Literature	1.00	1.10
Garnett's Selections in English Prose from Elizabeth to Victoria	1.50	1.65
Gayley's Classic Myths in English Literature	1.50	1.65
Gayley and Scott's Literary Criticism	1.25	1.40
Gummere's Handbook of Poetics	1.00	1.10
Hudson's Classical English Reader	1.00	1.10
Hudson's Essays on English, Studies in Shakespeare, etc.	.25	.27
Hudson's Life, Art, and Characters of Shakespeare. 2 vols. retail, cloth, $4.00; half morocco, $8.00		
Hudson's Text-book of Poetry	1.25	1.40
Hudson's Text-book of Prose	1.25	1.40
Kent's Shakespeare Note-Book	.60	.70
Lewis' Beginnings of English Literature	.90	.95
Minto's Characteristics of the English Poets	1.50	1.65
Minto's Manual of English Prose Literature	1.50	1.65
Painter's Elementary Guide to Literary Criticism	.90	.95
Phelps' Beginnings of the English Romantic Movement	1.00	1.10
Saintsbury's Loci Critici. Passages Illustrative of Critical Theory and Practice from Aristotle Downward	1.50	1.65
Sherman's Analytics of Literature	1.25	1.40
Smith's Synopsis of English and American Literature	.80	.90
Standard English Classics: 31 volumes now ready.		
Thayer's Best Elizabethan Plays	1.25	1.40
White's Philosophy of American Literature	.30	.35
White's Philosophy of English Literature	1.00	1.10
Winchester's Five Short Courses of Reading in English Literature	.40	.45

GINN & COMPANY Publishers

Outline on Webster's First Bunker

I. Introduction.
      A. Exordium — Patriotic Sentiment
             1
             2
             3
             4
             5

      B. Narration — Circumstances which
          occasion this address.
             6
             7

      C. Divisio — Treatment of the subject
                 indicated.
             8
             9
            10

II. Body.
      A. Address.
             12
             13
             14
             15
             16
             17

      B. Thoughts about the Battle.
             18
             19
             20
             21
             22